LONDON

Welcome to London

F. George Kay

Collins
Glasgow and London

Cover photographs
British Tourist Authority and Van Phillips

Photographs
Aerofilms
pp. 80–1

J. Allan Cash
pp. 22–3 (9, 10), 51, 53, 58, 65 (bottom), 69, 71, 76 (l.), 79 (bottom),
88–9, 90–1, 93, 98–9, 114–15 (top), 116, 116–17, 118–19, 120–1, 122–3,
124

British Tourist Authority
pp. 22–3 (4, 6), 28, 31, 61 (top l. and bottom), 74–5, 81, 94–5 (top), 100,
104–5 (top), 112–13 (top), 114–15 (bottom)

Colorsport
pp. 22–3 (1, 2)

Cooper-Bridgeman Library
p. 77

Keith Ellis
pp. 63 (bottom l.), 70 (rt), 78 (top), 79 (top), 85

Floracolour
pp. 33, 117

Van Phillips
pp. 22–3 (3, 7, 8), 30, 56, 61 (mid), 63 (top l.), 70 (l.), 73 (bottom), 78
(bottom), 78–9, 80, 82–3, 84, 86–7 (top), 92, 92–3, 96–7 (top), 102–3,
108–9, 110–11, 112–13 (bottom)

Pictor
pp. 65 (top), 76 (rt), 86–7 (bottom)

Robin Ward
pp. 22–3 (5), 32, 48, 57, 61 (top rt), 63 (mid l. and rt), 67, 73 (top l. and
rt), 74, 75, 82, 83, 84–5, 90, 91, 94–5 (bottom), 96–7 (bottom), 106–7
(top)

Whitbread Breweries/National Trust
pp. 104–5 (bottom)

Reg Wilson
pp. 106–7 (bottom)

Illustrations
pp. 4–9 Barry Rowe; pp. 100–1 Robin Ward

Maps
between pp. 60–76 M. and R. Piggott

First published 1980
Revised edition published 1984, 1988
Copyright © F. George Kay 1980
Published by William Collins Sons and Company Limited
Printed in Great Britain

Special printing for British Airways 1988
ISBN 0 00 447555 0

CONTENTS

Every effort has been made to give you an up-to-date text. Nevertheless the publisher can accept no responsibility for errors or ommissions, or for changes in detail.

London, first great city of the English-speaking peoples, financial heart of the Commonwealth, and cultural hub of Britain, is old, yet paradoxically as modern as today. If it is redolent with history it is not moribund in the stranglehold of its past. Never has there been a time when its citizens have not been ready to modernize the buildings and, although cathedrals, churches, palaces and state buildings have survived the past, there are no great architectural dinosaurs, their useful life long over. This thread of confidence in the future runs through the long story of Britain's capital and helps to explain its vitality, without contemptuous dismissal of prior contributions to its life. Modern buildings can be seen everywhere, yet they stand on ground plans drawn up centuries ago, and the winding lanes of the City, the old highways leading to the provinces, and the spacious squares of 18th-century gracious living remain largely as their originators intended.

The destiny of London as one of the world's greatest cities was assured when mankind discovered that the Mediterranean was not the centre of the world. Phoenician and Greek merchant seamen sailing past the Straits of Gibraltar into the Atlantic, Roman legions colonizing far beyond the Alps, and migrating tribes from Central Europe, widened the horizon to the edge of the Old World. The calm, broad estuary of the Thames with its tidal ebb and flow making navigation easy for more than 56km/35mi from the sea, brought these explorers to a landing and trading zone easily reached from the west coast of Europe, from Scandinavia to Spain.

Celtic migrants were probably the first to discover that after passing intermina-ble stretches of swampy land, fringed by dense forest, there were, at the head of the tidal waters, low hills of gravel on each side of the river, where the water was shallow enough to be forded at low tide. On the north side these founders of London built huts on two of the gravel outcrops – now known as Cornhill and Ludgate Hill. A few families chose a smaller mound of gravel on the other bank, to be known centuries later as Southwark.

No traces of these primitive communities have survived – except perhaps in the name of London. It is regarded as being derived from a Celtic word for a clan or tribal name *Londinos*, meaning the fierce ones. Their survival as a static community, rather than moving on as nomads, must have been due to their martial prowess. In this strange island they had discovered an easily defended area, near fertile soil, which was above all a convenient landing place for traders.

The first major battle for London was waged by Julius Caesar during his second invasion of Britain in 54 BC. His legions fought their way through Kent, constantly harassed by small groups of Belgic warriors. He was prevented from making a direct assault on the settlement, which he named *Londinium*, by swamps stretching far inland from the river's south bank between modern Greenwich and Battersea. Although a natural ford existed at Thorney Island (the modern Westminster), it was too much of a hazard for his heavily armed troops. Instead, Caesar crossed at Brentford and then moved north east in pursuit of his most formidable, adversaries, the Belgic Catuvellauni tribe, under their chief, Cassivellaunus. Before Caesar could destroy the enemy, rebellion in Gaul (France) demanded his

return to the mainland of Europe. If he could have remained in personal control London might have become a Roman strongpoint more than a century before it actually did.

That development took place in AD 43 when the Emperor Claudius sent his general Aulus Plautius to annex Britain for the Empire. Roman troops – accompanied by merchants and administrators to exploit the resources of the newly conquered colony – settled in a fortified zone on the east side of a stream (now known as Walbrook). It is believed they organized a river ferry, and possibly a pontoon bridge, leading directly to the site from the south side of the river.

Within a dozen years civilian enterprise had expanded the cluster of huts and modest defences into a collection of dwelling places, store rooms and stabling. Trade, under the protection of the Roman guards, increased steadily. Caesar had believed that Britain's ingots of tin were mined somewhere in the interior of the island, unaware that the metal was brought overland from the far west of Britain now that the new trading centre on the Thames had become the most profitable outlet.

Uncharacteristic laxity in constructing a strong military base brought its penalty. In AD 61, while the C-in-C of the Roman forces in Britain, Suetonius Paulinus, was pacifying North Wales, Boadicea, queen of the Iceni in East England, raised the forces of rebellion to avenge the brutal treatment of herself and her daughters by Roman officials. Legend exaggerated the total of the force she led south. It has been claimed that by the time she had sacked the Roman towns of Colchester and St Albans she had 250,000 men, women and children on the rampage, their target: London. What is certain is that the rebel mob far outnumbered the 10,000 Roman troops which Paulinus was able to rally through forced marches from every corner of the country. By then London had been captured and burned to the ground, its Roman citizens and all Britons working for them massacred. In the three sacked towns 70,000 colonists and their followers died, a figure which gives some idea of the size of the Roman population. Superior tactics brought the inevitable Roman revenge. Somewhere north of the ashes of the first Roman London the converging Roman legions trapped the ragged mass of Britons, loaded down with loot, and annihilated them.

Excavate deep enough into the ground beneath today's busy streets and the mechanical grabs reach the black layer of ashes left by this first Fire of London. The attack was perhaps as senseless as it was ultimately futile, but Boadicea remains London's first heroine, her story something that every London schoolchild learns. The bronze statue of her in her war chariot stands beside Westminster Bridge under the shadow of Big Ben; it defied the bombs of the 20th century and survives untouched.

London rose from the ashes, growing larger and more prosperous than ever. Defensive walls had been built. Within them was a Roman forum and the largest basilica, or town hall, outside Rome (on the site of the present Leadenhall Market, below which some remains of the original building were found in 1881).

By AD 130 London was the fifth largest town in the west of the Roman Empire. The town was minting its own coins by

the end of the 3rd century. In the 4th century, as a mark of Imperial regard, it was granted the title *Londinium Augusta*, London Majestic.

This was the twilight of the Roman Empire. Saxon pirates raiding unmolested in the English Channel were probing the Thames estuary. London remained inviolate behind her walls but overseas traders had to run the gauntlet of the sea rovers. In AD 410 Rome withdrew from Britain, leaving the citizens of London to defend themselves. They were constantly attacked, and as a result sent an appeal for military aid to Rome in AD 446. It was refused.

In common with the rest of south-east England, London lapsed into desolation, its churches and Roman administrative buildings destroyed, its trade almost nonexistent. Little is known about this chaotic period beyond the telltale traces of ashes above those of Boadicea's sacking of the town. Revival was slow, but by the early 7th century London had been restored as the chief town of the East Saxons. The first St Paul's cathedral was built in this period, paid for by Ethelbert, king of Kent, converted to Christianity in 597. He persuaded thousands of his subjects to reject their tribal gods and to replace their pagan temples with Christian churches. It is probable that under his influence the City began its tradition of church building. Remains of one Saxon church were discovered only after air-raid damage to St Brides in Fleet St. Below a number of church foundations, Saxon construction attributed to the 6th century was uncovered.

Little more than a century passed with a semblance of peace and prosperity for the Saxon town. Viking raiders attacked it in 839 and again in 851 in quick, vicious forays to intimidate the inhabitants and seize booty. Twenty years later the Danes, as the Vikings were by then known, temporarily occupied the City until Alfred the Great stemmed the invading forces and arranged a treaty which divided the country into Anglo-Saxon and Danish areas. In the ensuing political stability, Alfred set about restoring London. He repaired the half-ruined walls and appointed his son-in-law as governor. London withstood further assaults until the Danes, who had established their own community just across the river in Southwark, took over in 892. It was little more than a token occupation until the folkmoot (the assembly of the citizens of London) formally submitted to King Cnut (Canute), Danish conqueror of England.

Unlike his predecessors, Cnut realized the value of cooperation with his defeated enemies. He appointed Saxon administrators and gained the friendship of the ordinary people by sending large numbers of his troops back to Denmark. In London, administration was left in the hands of the folkmoot, the hustings (City of London court) and the City's aldermen. That independence has remained inviolate, and every attempt, ancient or modern, to weaken it, has been successfully resisted. Even today this tiny area (roughly a square mile) of a sprawling city has its own police force, its own court, and the monarch can enter only by permission of the Lord Mayor. Troops can march through with bayonets fixed only when formally permitted to do so.

Faced with the Norman invasion of 1066, Londoners prepared to resist occupation. They watched William the Con-

queror's troops set Southwark ablaze across the river, but were not intimidated. William calculated that an assault across the Thames would be futile. He marched his army 72km/45mi west and crossed the river at Wallingford, then wheeling east, he attacked London on its northern flank. Given the chance to submit as undefeated adversaries, Londoners agreed to peace. William confirmed the City's existing rights and soon enhanced the City's safety from attack by building the Tower of London and two other defensive towers. London had been conquered by an invader for the last time.

The Tower was also intended to serve as the sovereign's residence. The presence of the king within the boundaries of the City was sullenly accepted by the merchants of London, who regarded themselves, justifiably, as the real rulers of the City. Succeeding monarchs took the hint, and from the reign of Edward the Confessor onwards, the kings made Westminster their official residence.

The major enemy of the City, however, remained a lurking menace. In 1077 fire 'such as never was before since London was founded' swept across the huddle of wooden houses, the chronicler evidently unaware of the holocaust during the attack by Boadicea. In 1096 'the greatest and fairest part of the city' was burned to the ground. Then in 1136 came the Great Fire of London, as it was known until a still greater one broke out in 1666, this in turn dwarfed by the series of fire blitzes during the Second World War. After each conflagration Londoners cleared up the debris, rebuilt, and carried on.

From the 12th century onwards the financial resources and obstinate determination to maintain London's independence came largely from the merchant and craft guilds. They controlled the economic life of the City, nominated officials and supervised religious and social activities. The guilds became enormously wealthy, building magnificent halls for their meetings, paying for roads and bridges, running schools for their members' sons, and establishing standards of workmanship and commercial probity. Guilds, also known as livery companies because in the 14th century members began to wear a distinctive dress, still flourish today.

At present there are 84 City guilds, 12 of which are described as 'great'. Some 10,000 members are entitled to vote at elections of officers administering the City. The crafts and trades represented range from Air Pilots and Navigators to Basketmakers, from Fan Makers to Launderers. Many of their halls were damaged or destroyed during World War II, but most have been restored to their prior magnificence. Some can be visited by arrangement (details from the City of London Information Centre in St Paul's Churchyard). The most impressive are the halls of the Apothecaries, Fishmongers, Goldsmiths, Merchant Taylors, and Vintners.

The 12th century saw the City constructing streets and market places which remain on the map of today. In 1189 a law was passed requiring that ground floors of all houses be built of stone or brick, and roofs tiled or slated to minimize fire risk. The new London Bridge, built of stone, was completed in 1209. Clean drinking water was piped from the Tyburn stream to outlets around the City. Traders were grouped according to their wares in streets and squares. More people went to

live just beyond the City gates, with houses, shops and taverns stretching towards the village of Charing and the palace and abbey at Westminster.

The congestion of a rapidly increasing population crammed into an area originally intended as a small, strongly defended market town brought near-disaster in the 14th century. Black Death, the virulent disease considered to have been a variation of bubonic or pneumonic plague, reached the West of England in the autumn of 1348. Wool merchants travelling to London brought the disease with them. In November the first cases in the City occurred. By Christmas deaths were averaging 200 a day, and the epidemic continued for three months. An estimated 17,000 people died, about half the City's population. The survivors, if they had the resources, fled to rural areas. Years passed before the City returned to normality. But within three generations Londoners stood on the brink of a glittering future.

Influence and prosperity beyond the imagination of the merchants and craftsmen of medieval London became assured (though none realized it at the time) with the discovery of America by Columbus in 1492. Up till then European trade had centred on the City States of Italy – Florence, Venice, Genoa. But London, on the western edge of the Old World, was the obvious mercantile depot for development and trade with the New World, challenged only by Spain which, due to its monopolistic policy, lost the chance to handle the movement of merchandise and human beings from all Europe across the ocean. And London steadily rose in status as the first centre of global communication – an eminence it

has retained today as the busiest junction of worldwide air routes.

All this time the royal and religious centre of Westminster was growing rapidly. The Romans reputedly had a small military post there. In the 7th century a church was built, consecrated to St Peter. A few years before the Norman Conquest, Edward the Confessor had begun the construction of an immense church. It lasted for two centuries, when Henry III began the Abbey as it stands today. It took nearly three centuries to complete. Alongside the Abbey, on a site now occupied by the Houses of Parliament, Edward the Confessor also built his palace. Houses went up for state administrators, and by the 14th century Westminster was developing as the royal and governmental centre of the nation. Under the Tudors, wealthy and aristocratic citizens began to leave the City for more spacious and pleasant houses along the north bank of the river and in Westminster itself.

Two communities were linking to create Greater London, with a population during the reign of Elizabeth I of about 200,000. During the 17th century further development spread the town northwards from the Thames to absorb villages and farmland in Covent Garden, Bloomsbury and Marylebone. This rapid expansion was halted only by the outbreak of plague in 1665, which exacted a fearful toll in the congested areas and caused thousands to flee to the countryside. For the stricken City further disaster arrived in the Great Fire of 1666, which burned for five days, destroying St Paul's, 89 parish churches, 400 streets and lanes and 13,200 houses, leaving 100,000 people without a home or place of work. Once again the resilience

of London had normal life restored in a phenomenally brief period. The destruction caused by the fire also produced London's greatest architectural genius, Sir Christopher Wren, whose work can be seen everywhere, though his grandiose plan for a completely new City of London was rejected.

Over all these centuries, the area south of the river remained unimpressive. Until 1729 there was no bridge across the Thames below Putney apart from London Bridge, which originally was too narrow to allow heavy wagons to pass. Consequently all merchandise to and from the south of England had to be off-loaded on the south bank. To Londoners this was a 'foreign' district, as indeed it had been since the invading Danes had settled there. It was famous, or infamous, for its prisons, taverns, brothels and places of amusement. Little or no control existed over the hordes of inhabitants and the visitors arriving for business or pleasure, and the area continued as a shabby though useful offshoot of the community north of the river, until the devastation of the Second World War presented the opportunity to create a new and attractive area of London.

During the 18th century Britain's international trade increased enormously and, with the extension of the docks making London the world's largest port, the City spread to the east, mostly with housing for workers, which rapidly degenerated into slums. In contrast, the area beyond the City and Westminster was developed with pleasant squares and attractive houses for the prosperous middle class. By the end of the century the population had grown to 850,000 and, in the 1900s, when London was so vast that

it had become a county, there were four and a half million Londoners. Little of architectural worth emerged during the Victorian Age, apart from the Houses of Parliament – an enforced project after most of the old Palace of Westminster had been destroyed by fire in 1834 and the development in Kensington of an area of museums and luxurious town houses.

Nor can the 20th century claim that it has added to the architectural splendour of the capital. After the city endured the greatest blaze of all in the fire raids of World War II, in which many hundreds of buildings in every part of the capital, from Buckingham Palace and the Houses of Parliament to the docks and slums of the East End, were damaged or destroyed, the most commendable feature of reconstruction was the painstaking restoration of all that was good from the past. For the rest, the innate practicality of Londoners demanded that new building should be a contribution to the business and commercial life of the capital. As always, though conscious of the past, London had its eyes on the future.

The visitor will see London as a welcoming blend of glorious past and stimulating present, perhaps unsurpassed by any other of the world's great cities. The array of its interests may bewilder him to explore its streets and buildings, and to get to know its friendly people. They are proud of their city, glad to share it with the visitor, claiming, as the Elizabethan poet Edmund Spenser did four centuries ago:

At length they all to mery London came,
To mery London, my most kyndly Nurse.

ARRIVAL IN LONDON

Travel Documents

A valid passport (or proof of identity from Citizens of EEC countries). A visa is not required of US citizens, nationals of the British Commonwealth and most European countries. Health certificates are normally required only by those arriving from Asia, Africa and South America. In common with other countries Britain does not require a certificate of vaccination against smallpox.

By Air

Heathrow Airport, 22km/14mi west of the centre of London, is directly linked to the Underground station by a moving walkway. Journey time to Piccadilly Circus is about 45 mins. Trains run from 0500-2350 (0645-2350 Sun.). Airline buses to all major hotel areas and Victoria Coach Station maintain frequent services 0630-2130. Flightline 767 coaches at 30 min. intervals to Victoria, stops at Kensington and Hyde Park Corner. Taxis available at airport terminals.

Gatwick Airport, 48km/30mi south of the centre of London, is directly linked by British Rail to Victoria. Journey time by Gatwick Express is 30 mins. British Caledonian and some other airlines' passengers can check in at the B.C. Air Terminal at Victoria Station. Flightline 777 coaches non-stop hourly to Victoria.

Luton Airport, 51km/32mi north of London. Luton Flyer train and coach service takes 45 mins. to London (St. Pancras). Flightline 757 coaches at 30 min. intervals to Victoria stops at Finchley Rd, Baker St., Marble Arch and Hyde Park Corner.

Stansted, 55km/34mi north east of the centre of London, is adjacent to the M11 motorway to London. Most charter flight operators provide a bus service. By rail, Bishop's Stortford to Liverpool St. (38 mins.), with taxis to and from airport. Green Line and Flightline coaches link with main flight arrivals and run to Victoria. (A direct rail service to Liverpool St. is due to be completed by 1990.)

By Sea

British Rail boat trains connect with ship arrivals: **Charing Cross** from Dover, Folkestone, Ramsgate. **Liverpool Street** from Felixstowe, Harwich. **Victoria** from Newhaven. **Waterloo** from Southampton. **Fenchurch Street** from Tilbury.

By Road

All motorways and A roads from the provinces to London are linked with the North and South Circular Roads, and the M25 orbital road.

By Rail

British Rail **main-line terminals** for routes from ports, provinces, Scotland and Wales are:

Charing Cross (S and SE England). Buses in Strand. Three Underground systems serving all central districts direct.
Euston (Midlands, NW England and Scotland). Buses to all parts from Euston Rd. Underground runs direct to Tottenham Court Rd, Piccadilly Circus, *etc.*
Fenchurch Street (Tilbury). Buses just north of station in main street. Underground Tower Hill to Charing Cross, *etc.*
King's Cross (N England and Scotland). Buses to all parts from Euston Rd. Two. Underground systems, one Inner Circle serving edge of Central London, the other direct to Holborn, Leicester Sq., *etc.*
Liverpool Street (E England). Buses outside station entrance. Two Underground systems, one Inner Circle for edge of Central London, the other for Tottenham Court Rd, Oxford Circus, *etc.*
to Tottenham Court Rd, Oxford Circus, *etc.*
Paddington (W England and Wales). Buses outside station entrance. Two Underground systems, one Inner Circle serving edge of Central London, the other to Kensington, Oxford Circus, *etc.*
St Pancras (Midlands and NW). Buses in Euston Rd. Underground as for King's Cross (above).
Victoria (SE and S England). Buses outside station. Three Underground systems.
Waterloo (S and SW England). Buses outside station. Two Underground systems, one to Charing Cross, Piccadilly Circus, Oxford Circus, Baker St., *etc*, the other to Leicester Sq., *etc.*

Information

All main-line terminals and Victoria Coach Station have enquiry bureaus. In the Underground station ticket hall at Heathrow there are facilities for currency exchange and details of all transit facilities to London. At the tourist information centre in Victoria railway station forecourt information on accommodation, travel, *etc*, is available.

ACCOMMODATION

Many new hotels, in both luxury and popular categories, have opened in recent years. Within the Greater London area there are more than 800 hotels and guest houses officially regarded as meeting required standards. Nevertheless, during the summer vacation season, demand is very heavy, and visitors are well advised to book in advance through a travel agency, worldwide hotel group, or by written application (at least six weeks in advance) to the London Visitor and Convention Bureau, Information Centre, Victoria Station, London SW1.

Hotels with four or more bedrooms normally display details of overnight charges in the reception foyer or at the entrance.

Hotels in districts W1 and SW1 are mostly in the luxury class with an international reputation for cuisine, comfort and service. Many in Kensington, Chelsea, Pimlico, Bayswater and Bloomsbury are less expensive and range from small and modest to large and impressive. The districts mentioned are all within a few minutes by Underground or bus from the main centres of tourist interest. Beyond this inner zone, rates are proportionately lower in the suburbs but sightseeing will involve time and money spent on travel.

Most of the newly-built or modernized hotels in all categories have rooms with private baths (more usual than showers).

Advertised charges usually quote terms for a single or double room, with or without bath, for bed and breakfast (with choice of Continental or full English breakfast); weekly terms for full board (breakfast, lunch, dinner), or half board (breakfast and evening meal).

All hotels have to charge Value Added Tax (VAT is a variable tax, shown separately on a bill for services, but included in the purchase price of goods). Many hotels add a service charge (10 percent or 12½ percent on the bill less VAT) in lieu of gratuities. The service charge can be to the guest's advantage as tipping members of the staff individually is likely to work out to 15 percent. In assessing the cost of your stay it is important to check whether the stated terms cover VAT and service, and also such extras as bedroom fire, radio, TV, *etc.*

Charges for children between 5 and 14 are usually slightly reduced even though they occupy separate rooms and have full meals. A cot, or crib, for a young child in the parents' room and 'child's helpings' at mealtimes can usually be arranged for about half or two-thirds of the adult rate.

In districts on the fringe of the West End, and particularly around the main rail termini, are numerous small establishments usually described as private hotels.

Their classification is more accurately boarding house. Charges are modest. Standards vary, and it is advisable personally to inspect the room and general facilities before making an actual reservation unless a friend has recommended it.

London Homestead Services, approved by the LVCB, offer the chance to stay with a friendly London family in well situated, clean, quiet rooms with all facilities and easy access to Central London. Bed and breakfast only. Minimum of 3 days' stay. Offices at 154 Warwick Road, W14 8PS for enquiries by post, or phone 602 9851 in office hours, 949 4455 evenings and weekends.

Advance planning is wise, ideally with a booking made at least six weeks in advance. Write giving date of arrival and desired duration to the Information Unit of the LVCB, 26 Grosvenor Gardens, SW1 0DU enclosing a reply-paid self-addressed envelope. A deposit will be payable on the accepted offer. For overseas visitors there is also the British Tourist Authority, Thames Tower, Black's Rd, W6, which can supply lists of all grades of hotels in London and the suburbs. Details and a booking form will be sent if a reply paid self-addressed envelope is enclosed.

Overseas offices of the BTA can also provide this information. They operate in all principal overseas countries. For Commonwealth and USA residents the addresses are: Australia: 171 Clarence St., Sydney NSW 2000. Canada: 94 Cumberland St., Suite 600, Toronto, Ontario M5R 3N3. New Zealand: Box 3655, Wellington. USA: John Hancock Center, Suite 3320, 875N, Michigan Ave., Chicago, Ill 60611; Plaza of the Americas, 750 North Tower LB346, Dallas, Texas 75201; 612 South Flower St., Los Angeles CA90017; 680 Fifth Ave., New York NY10019.

Members of the Youth Hostels Association can stay in five hostels in London: Holland Park, Kensington; 84 West Hill, Highgate N6; 36 Carter Lane EC4; Hampstead Heath, NW3, and 38 Bolton Gardens SW5.

GETTING AROUND LONDON

Underground Trains

Ten systems cover the whole of London and the suburbs. All lines pass through interchange stations. Maps in the station foyer, on the platform, and in every coach indicate where a change of train is necessary (see map pp. 32-3). The Underground is the quickest form of travel for journeys of more than 3km/2mi, but for shorter distances it is usually better to use road transport.

Tickets must be bought from machines or the booking office before starting the journey. At most stations, tickets are checked by a machine: the ticket is inserted in a slot and ejected as the turnstile is unlocked.

British Rail Trains

Details can be obtained at all main terminals, and at British Rail travel centres at 12 Lower Regent St. SW1; 407 Oxford St. W1; 170b Strand WC2; 14 Kingsgate Parade, Victoria St. SW1; and 87 King William St. EC4 (Mon.-Fri. 0900-1700).

Buses

All red buses carry the route number and destination at the front and rear. Bus stops (except request stops) have panels on the post to indicate route numbers, their destination and route. Tickets are bought (or special tickets shown) on boarding from the conductor or driver. Most buses have separate entry and exit doors. To simplify fare rates London is divided into bus and underground zones. For most places of interest bus zone 1 (Central) and zone 2 (Inner) will be the maximum fare involved. Within the Central zone the maximum fare is 50p. Children under 5 travel free; under 14: 15p, 14 and 15 the same reduction, but they must hold a child photocard, available at travel centres, Underground stations, and Post Offices.

A special group of buses with limited stops is numbered from 500 to 513. They leave Victoria, Waterloo, Liverpool St. and London Bridge stations on weekdays covering most principal streets.

Special Tickets

The London Explorer ticket available for 1, 3, 4 or 7 days gives unlimited travel on buses and the Underground, including to and from Heathrow. It includes discount vouchers on attractions such as the Zoo and Madame Tussauds.

One Day Travel Cards are valid for an unlimited number of bus journeys after 0930 Mon.-Fri. and any time Sat. and Sun. They can also be used on the Underground in most of the Central, Inner and Outer areas.

One Day Capital Cards are available for any period from 7 days. They provide the same facilities as the One Day Travel card plus travel outside the London zones. They are sold at stations. A passport photo must be handed in with the application.

Bus and Coach Sightseeing Tours

London Transport sightseeing tour. Double deck bus (open top in summer) on 30km/18mi. tour lasting about 1½ hrs.

Route includes Westminster Abbey, the Houses of Parliament, St. Paul's, and the Tower. A qualified Tourist Board guide provides a commentary; on some buses a French and German commentary is available. Frequent departures from Victoria, Piccadilly Circus (Haymarket), Marble Arch, and Baker St. station. Pay as you board the bus, but there is a price reduction if tickets are bought in advance at any LVCB information centre or London Transport office.

Culture Bus. Continuous on-off tour service at ½ hr. intervals on 30km/18mi route stopping at all the sightseeing places in Central London. Passengers pay a flat rate and can alight and rejoin the next bus to arrive at their chosen stop. Enquire at travel agents or LVCB offices for convenient boarding point.

Cityrama tour. 2-hr. circular tour with recorded commentary in eight languages. Boarding at Grosvenor Gardens, Victoria; Broad Sanctuary, Westminster; and Trafalgar Sq. For reservations and times enquire at travel agents or LVCB offices. Or phone 720 6663.

London Pride sightseeing tour. 1½ hrs. tour of most of the sights in Westminster and the City. Tours start every ½ hr. from Coventry St., Piccadilly. 25 percent discount for passengers buying tickets in advance from National Express agents or at Victoria coach station.

London Crusader sightseeing tours all have guides and range from half-day, full day or evening trips. There is also a 4-hour tour of Sunday London. Departures from Wilton Rd coach station, Victoria, with pick-up points at many London hotels. Enquiries and bookings at any travel agent linked to National Express. Phone information on 437 0124 or 730 0202.

Green Line coaches run between central London and the suburbs and towns in the Home Counties. Terminals are at Victoria coach station, Eccleston Bridge SW1; and Buckingham Palace Rd SW1. Limited stops in London. Enquiries 668 7261.

Taxi Cabs

A yellow sign 'for hire' is illuminated when a cab is available, and it must normally stop and pick up passengers wishing to be driven to a destination within the Metropolitan district (all of Inner London and major part of Greater London area). The fare is shown on the meter along with a notice of any supplementary charges. The usual gratuity is 15-20 percent of the fare.

Radio-linked taxis and the so-called minicabs must be ordered by phone. Hotels have the numbers and they are also in the Yellow Pages. It is as well to agree the approximate fare before taking one of these taxis.

Motoring Organizations

If overseas visitors, bringing their own cars to the UK, are members of a motoring organization in their own country, which is affiliated to the Fédération Internationale de l'Automobile (FIA) or the Commonwealth Motoring Conference (CMC), they can make use of the reciprocal facilities provided by the two British clubs, AA and RAC: **Automobile Association** Fanum House, Basingstoke, Hants RG21 2EA. **Royal Automobile Club** 89 Pall Mall, London SW1. Both clubs maintain offices at all ports of entry for car-carrying ferries.

Rules of the Road

The information below is an outline of regulations and laws, and is not intended as a complete survey. For official information consult *The Highway Code*, obtainable at booksellers.

Roads are classified M (motorways), A (main roads), B (minor roads). R indicates a ring road round London and other cities.

Signs Warning signs are triangles with a red border, with the nature of the warning in black. Order signs are circular with a red border, with the nature of the order in black. Information signs are rectangular or circular, with a blue background. Direction signs are rectangular: blue on or near motorways, green or white on other roads.

Road markings White lines: solid single or double line across road indicates stop; triangle and broken double line mean yield right-of-way; broken lines along the road indicate traffic lane and centre line; double line in centre of road prohibits crossing; double line with one line broken indicates no crossing if the nearer line is unbroken; crossing permitted when road is clear if broken line is nearer. Yellow lines at side of road: single, no waiting during working day; double, no waiting during working day and at additional times. Check the times of no waiting, shown on nearby signs.

Drive on the left and overtake on the right. Maximum speed in built-up areas with street lamp posts is 30 miles per hour (48.3kph). Outside built-up areas and on motorways, speed limits vary according to maximum speed signs, usual maximum is 70 miles per hour (112.7kph) on motorways and dual carriageways, and 60 miles per hour (95.6kph) on other roads unless a lower limit is indicated by signs.

Lights must be used in the period half an hour after sunset to half an hour before sunrise. They must also be used in daylight hours when visibility is poor.

Horns must not be used in a built-up area between 2330 and 0700 hours or at any time when the vehicle is stationary.

Driving licence A current driving licence issued in the visitor's own country is usually valid, or an International Circulation Permit is obtainable at the port of entry. Minimum age for driving a car or motorcycle larger than 50cc is 17, for mopeds or motor-assisted cycles 16.

Pedestrians have right-of-way at zebra crossings with flashing yellow beacons and black and white road panels; in the area marked with zig-zag lines before and beyond the crossing no car may park or stop for passenger to enter or alight. At pedestrian crossings with traffic light signals, steady or flashing amber means give precedence to any pedestrian. Uniformed patrols showing a 'Stop-Children' sign operate between the hours of 0800 and 1730. Drivers must stop.

Third-party insurance is compulsory.

Tyres It is an offence to drive with tyres which are not properly inflated or have a severe cut. The tread pattern must have depth of *at least* 1 mm throughout.

Safety belts The wearing of seat belts by driver and front seat passenger in a car is required by law. Children 1-14 in the front seat must wear an approved child restraint or adult belt.

Parking Parking in most streets is permitted only at meters, usually for a period of two hours. Spaces at parking meters are hard to come by. Off-street parking in underground and multi-story parks is indicated by a white P on a blue background; most car parks make a minimum charge for two hours, weekly rates are available. In some residential areas parking is restricted to local residents. Vehicles illegally parked may be ticketed or wheel-clamped and towed away by the police to compounds. (Apply at nearest police station for information as to where the car has been taken.)

Fixed penalties for driving offences. Non-endorsable offences (i.e. not entered on the driving licence), involve the issue of a ticket, carrying a penalty of £12, payable within 28 days. Non-payment and no request for a court hearing: the penalty is then registered as a fine and increased to £18. Endorsable offences bring entry on the driving licence. A total of 12 points or more means prosecution and possible disqualification. A ticket for an endorsable offence carries a penalty of £24 and is issued only after a police officer has checked that the driving licence will not as a result carry 12 or more endorsements. Below the total of 12 endorsements: failure to pay the penalty within 28 days or request a court hearing means the penalty is increased to £36 and registered as a fine.

Drink or drug offences. A uniformed

police constable can require a driver to take a breathalyzer test. After arrest there can be blood or urine tests. Unfitness to drive is with a breath alcohol level higher than 35mg per 100 ml, equivalent to a blood alcohol level of 80mg per 100 ml. Heavy fines and or imprisonment may be imposed on offenders.

Helmets for motor cycles and moped riders and pillion passengers. Failure to wear safety helmets involves the same penalty as described above for ticketed non-endorsable offences − £12.

More serious offences. Exceeding the speed limit, driving without due care and attention, reckless or dangerous driving, causing injury or death by driving carry heavy fines, and in some categories imprisonment. Endorsement of the driving licence and disqualification for a period commensurate with the severity of the offences are the likely decision of the courts.

Accidents It is a driver's duty to stop and report an accident involving any other vehicle, most domesticated animals, persons, or roadside property, to anyone who has reasonable grounds to request name, address, and details of insurance policy, or to a police station within 24 hours. The driver of any vehicle involved in an accident should note the registration number of any other vehicle involved or in the vicinity, take names and addresses of witnesses, and make a sketch of the area where the accident occurred.

If injury has occurred dial 999 from the nearest telephone and ask for an ambulance and police. If there is no phone near the accident, ask any motorist to drive to the nearest phone. Do not go too far from the accident yourself.

Cycles

For the newcomer the use of a bicycle demands steady nerves and a good knowledge of every district visited. Dial-a-Bike (828 4040), 18 Gillingham St. SW1, and Bike UK Ltd. (839 2111), Lower Robert St. WC2, rent cycles by the day or week. The Cyclists Touring Club has an enquiry office at 13 Spring St. W2.

Waterborne Travel

The Thames offers trips on launches between the piers at Westminster, Festival Hall, Charing Cross, the Tower, Greenwich and the Thames Flood Barrier; and between Westminster Bridge, Putney, Kew, Richmond and Hampton Court (summer only).

Trips on the Regent's Canal ply between Little Venice, Paddington (bus or Underground Warwick Ave) and Camden Lock, passing the Zoo, and return. A waterbus service runs between Little Venice and the Zoo (April−Oct.).

FOOD AND DRINK

A minor revolution has occurred in London in recent years in the vast improvement in catering facilities − both in the variety and number of eating places. It is now misleading to suggest that any district in the capital is better than others. Intense competition and individual enterprise have resulted in many places off the well-known streets and outside the central area gaining a reputation for good food and service.

In the vicinity of Piccadilly, Park Lane, Hyde Park and Knightsbridge are the most luxurious establishments, with international reputations and prices to match. But these areas also have many modest eating places, and Soho, with its numerous restaurants offering ethnic fare, is only a few minutes' walk away. Chelsea has several good modern restaurants, many as popular for décor and entertainment as for food. Covent Garden is a rewarding district for anyone willing to discover the moderately priced small places flourishing there.

Restaurants offering foreign food have proliferated. Within 2km/1¼mi of Piccadilly Circus there are restaurants specializing in Chinese, Indian, Greek, Spanish, Japanese, Scandinavian, Russian, Hungarian, Swiss, Mexican, Jewish and Arabic dishes. The trio of established high-quality cuisines − French, Italian, and English − hold their own, and restaurants in the luxury class specialize in them. A few restaurants in Mayfair and Covent Garden feature American menus.

All reputable restaurants and cafés, except for those where money is no problem to the clientele, display a menu outside. Quoted prices should be assessed against any extras mentioned in small print. Meals are subject to the addition of Value Added Tax (VAT is a variable tax, shown separately on a bill for services, but included in the purchase price of goods) and there may also be cover and service charges. Any small change from paying the bill is usually left on the table. Where there is no service charge the normal tip for satisfactory service is 10−15 percent.

The majority of restaurants (not cafés) are licensed to provide alcoholic drinks with a meal; some without a licence will send out for them. In hotels residents may order alcoholic drinks at any time of the day with or without food. Open hours vary slightly from pub to pub, the legal requirement being that there is a maximum opening period of nine hours per day, with a minimum break of two and a half hours in the afternoon. The usual opening hours are between 1100–1430 and 1730–2300 weekdays; 1200–1400 and 1900–2230 Sundays.

For economy, good service and well-cooked food there is a simple rule: leave the popular thoroughfare and look around the adjacent side streets. Prices are lower because overheads are lower, and, as there is less chance of attracting the passerby, the owner tries harder to please. The menu outside and the general atmosphere within should indicate whether the little place tucked away in a mews or byway, even on the first floor above a shop, is a real find. Probably even cheaper, though the menu will not be so varied, are the self-service establishments. These are found in the busy streets and squares and they rely on large numbers of people taking quick meals.

Most hotels welcome nonresidents for meals. Thus it is possible to sample the cuisine of world-famous hotels such as the Savoy, Claridges, the Ritz, the London Hilton, the Inn on the Park, and so on, without being in the financial bracket of the residents. Lots of modest hotels in Bloomsbury, Kensington, and around the main-line terminals provide well-cooked meals, usually at lower prices than in restaurants. They are less crowded at peak hours and can be recommended for family parties. The selection of dishes is limited, but they are changed daily.

For local atmosphere or an inexpensive and quick lunch, try one of London's 7000 public houses. Some of the larger pubs have a separate restaurant with waiter service. The run-of-the-mill pub offers counter service whereby the customer orders his dish at the bar and either eats it there or takes it over to a handy table. The variety of dishes may be limited, but helpings are generous and prices lower than in the average restaurant. Most pubs can offer a bowl of soup and a selection of main dishes. It is customary, but not essential, to order an alcoholic drink as well. Regrettably licensing laws forbid the presence of children under the age of 14 in bars. This ban does not apply to a room set apart for meals at a table. Alcoholic drinks may not be sold to or bought by persons under 18, or consumed by them. Sixteen–18 year olds may have beer or cider with a meal served at a table.

Typical dishes are steak and kidney pie, shepherd's pie, sausages and mashed potatoes, various stewed meats with vegetables. In summer, cold meats and salads are usually available, and there are always sandwiches, generous quantities of bread and cheese and cold meat pies.

Tipping is not expected, but the barmaid or barman will not take it amiss if you offer a drink. Only pubs in districts where there are theatres and other evening entertainments serve bar meals in the evening.

Steak houses mainly form a part of a chain and they have gained the reputation for producing the same standard of quality and service in each of their establishments. The uncooked weight of the steak is usually mentioned on the menu, and prices include vegetables or salad. Prices are on the high side of moderate.

Large department stores often have restaurants and cafés within their premises and charge surprisingly modest prices for meals and snacks, the policy being that providing food and refreshment is good public relations and attracts people to the store. They tend to be patronized by shoppers and family groups; many offer small portions for children or special children's dishes.

Hamburger cafés are found in every district, and the English branches of the American chains serve the highest quality. Elsewhere quality varies, but price is a clue to what one can expect. In the evenings mobile stalls selling hamburgers and hot dogs are to be found parked in traffic-free streets and squares. Some caution is wise here, as standards of quality and hygiene vary greatly.

Sandwich and pizza bars abound everywhere; the food can be eaten on the premises or taken away. Sandwiches are usually freshly prepared on the premises, with coffee, tea and soft drinks available. Sandwich bars are very popular with London's working population and at lunchtime they are crowded.

Many of the parks have cafés and restaurants. The Cake House in St James's Park is excellent for morning coffee or afternoon tea. In Hyde Park there are two modern restaurants at either end of the Serpentine. Kensington Gardens has a refreshment kiosk near the children's playground. Regent's Park has an elegant restaurant and a cafeteria. In the Victoria Embankment Gardens there is an open-air café near the bandstand for enjoying lunchtime concerts.

Rather sadly for traditionalists, this tea-drinking nation has lost the scores of cafés established more than 70 years ago, bringing the comment from Edward VII, 'I like Mr Lyons; he feeds my people well'. Coffee bars have taken over and are found in every street They offer attractive cakes and pastries to go with the coffee, but quality can vary and a simple precaution is to check that there is an espresso machine or percolators for making 'real' coffee on the premises. A great advantage of the coffee bar is that it is open from morning till late at night.

Below is a selection of **restaurants** in the main sightseeing districts. They offer quality meals at a moderate price. Most welcome children. Days and times of opening are shown.

West End and Soho

Café crêperie, 27 Wardour St. W1. Savoury crêpes, side salads, ice cream. Daily 1000–2000.

Chicago Pizza Pie Factory, 17 Hanover St. W1. American-style deep-dish pizzas. Daily 1200–2330.

Cranks, 8 Marshall St. W1 (branches at 17 Gt. Newport St. WC2, 9 Tottenham St. W1, Unit No. 11, Covent Garden, WC2). Health foods served in a host of appetizing dishes. Daily 1000–23000 (times at branches vary).

Harry's, 19 Kingly St. W1. Simple English food, all home cooked. Nice for children as it is just behind Hamley's Regent St. toy shop. Mon.–Fri. 1000–1800.

Kettners, 29 Romilly St. W1. Famous Soho restaurant offering a variety of foods from pizzas, burgers, and sandwiches to multi-course meals. Daily 1200–2400.

Little Akropolis, 10 Charlotte St. W1. Authentic Greek food at moderate charges. Weekdays 1200–2200 (Sat. evenings only).

Pappagalli's, 7 Swallow St. W1. US-style pizzas, pasta dishes, and salads. Weekdays 1200–1500 and 1715–2400.

Swiss Centre, Leicester Sq. W1. Four different restaurants; the Rendezvous is inexpensive, with burgers, frankfurters and other Swiss meat dishes. Children welcomed. Daily 1200–2400.

West Central and Covent Garden

Food for Thought, 31 Neal St. WC2. Vegetarian menu with pastas, soups, salads, hot dishes. Daily 1200–2000.

The Happy Garden, 47 Charing Cross Rd WC2. Attractive Chinese restaurant at the gates to London's Chinatown in Gerrard St. and Lisle St., all offering the best value for money of any establishment in the West End. Most open daily 1200–2400 and later.

Joe Allen, 13 Exeter St. WC2. Famous as a corner of New York in London. Soups, spare ribs, burgers and salads.

Lyons Corner House, Strand, WC2. Huge restaurant re-opened with its pre-war attraction of every kind of snack or full meal at popular prices. Children specially catered for. Daily 0900–2400.

National Gallery Restaurant, Trafalgar Sq. WC2. Good food at modest prices, with menu changed daily, but always

including its famous sausages. Weekdays 1000–1700, Sun. 1400–1700.

Westminster and Chelsea

L.A. Cafe, 163 Knightsbridge SW1. Good for children who in the early evening can make their own pizzas. Menu with American, Mexican and European specialities. Daily 1200–2200.

Tate Gallery Restaurant, Tate Gallery, Millbank SW1. Traditional English dishes prepared from authentic old recipes. Weekdays 1000–1700.

Three Lanterns, 5 Panton St. SW1. Roast beef, lamb cutlets, goulash, etc. and good salads. Children's portions. Daily 1145–2300.

Kensington

Geale's Fish Restaurant, 2 Farmer St. W8. Old established fish and chip restaurant. Children welcome. Tues.–Sat. 1200–1500 and 1800–2300.

Steamboat Charley's, 205 Church St. W8. Another popular fish restaurant, this one offering both English and American dishes. Weekdays 1800–2330.

City and East End

Blooms, 90 Whitechapel High St. E1. Best-known kosher restaurant in London. Lavish portions. Sun.–Fri. 1100–2130. Closed Jewish holidays.

Quayside Restaurant, 1 St. Katherine's Way E1. Brand new establishment serving traditional English lunch on Sundays. Daily 1000–2000.

South of the Thames

The Dining Room, 1 Cathedral St. E1. Vegetarian and wholefood cooking of appetizing and unusual dishes. Tues.–Fri. 1230–1430 and 1900–2200.

Public Houses

Pubs can be relied upon for good standards of hygiene and service. The following selection is based on taverns of interest to visitors on account of their historical appeal or because they have a reputation for 'character'.

Anchor, Bankside SE1. A riverside pub with a balcony over the water; it was known to Shakespeare, though it was largely rebuilt in 1775.

Cock Inn, 22 Fleet St. EC4. Patronized by Dickens in his days as a young journalist. Now the favourite pub of Fleet St. newsmen.

Dickens Inn, St Katharine's Dock E1. Part of an old brewery and now a centre for yachtsmen using the St Katharine's Dock marina and yacht basin.

Dirty Dick's, 202 Bishopsgate EC2. Named after an 18th-century miser. Many relics of this notorious eccentric.

George Inn, 77 Borough High St. SE1. The only surviving galleried inn in

London. It was a terminus for the stage coaches to the south coast.

Jack Straw's Castle, Hampstead Heath NW3, stands on the highest point of the Heath with views across London to the Surrey hills. Washington Irving knew it when he was at the US legation in London.

Mayflower, 117 Rotherhithe St. SE16. Thameside pub with traditional links with the Pilgrim Fathers.

Old Cheshire Cheese, Wine Office Court, Fleet St. EC4. An unspoiled City tavern, with much the same menu as Dr. Johnson and Oliver Goldsmith enjoyed here.

Pindar of Wakefield, 328 Gray's Inn Rd WC1. Sixteenth-century tavern which maintains the old-time custom of robust and earthy entertainment.

Prospect of Whitby, 57 Wapping Wall E1. London's oldest riverside pub – 600 years old. Both Turner and Whistler painted river scenes from its balcony.

Sherlock Holmes, 10 Northumberland Ave WC2. A re-creation of the famous detective's rooms in Baker Street; mementos of the stories and their author.

Spaniards, Hampstead Heath NW3. Ancient tavern (the toll house survives) once patronized by highwaymen who accosted travellers on the lonely heath.

Dinner and Entertainment

London's after dark entertainment varies from the spectacular and expensive to the popular – there for the price of a drink and a sandwich. Casinos are very strictly controlled, and advertising is not permitted beyond a discreet name-plate at the door. Membership is essential, or an introduction by a member. Joining usually requires 48 hours' notice. The management of reputable hotels will assist would-be gamblers with names and addresses.

At the other end of the scale are the scores of pubs which have added live music, variety acts and discos to their normal services. Many wine bars have opened, and these serve hot and cold food as well as providing music and a few variety acts. Look for these places in Soho and Chelsea or check the frequently changing attractions in *Time Out*.

Night clubs invariably require membership, but it is usually a formality of applying 24 or 48 hours in advance and paying a nominal fee. Clubs enjoying publicity in the gossip columns offer meals, often the best anywhere in London, and at prices to match. Cocktails and champagne are the virtually standard drinks. The cabaret acts are top-liners. The spending spree can go on to 0300.

For those not in the big spenders class there are several night-time places offering very good value for money. Check the classified advertisements in the London dailies and evenings or in *Time Out* for details. The undermentioned are well established and have a reputation to maintain.

Astoria, 157 Charing Cross Rd WC2. Stage entertainment and dinner; periodically extended runs of top-line groups and variety acts.

Cafe de Paris, 3 Coventry St. WC2. A generation ago one of the most famous clubs in London. Excellent music for dancing. Patrons are expected to be dressed up for a special occasion. Open to 0300.

Empire Suite, 161 Tottenham Court Rd WC1. Popular with those who enjoy dancing whatever their age. Rhythms from the 1930's right up to this month.

Hammersmith Palais, 242 Shepherd's Bush Rd W6. Huge ballroom with the big band sound. No problems about membership and a chance to join with real Londoners enjoying themselves.

Hippodrome, Charing Cross Rd WC2. Dine, dance and watch the current variety and pop stars. A reasonable standard of dress expected.

100 Club, 100 Oxford St. W1. Blues, rock and jazz, with a different attraction each night. Moderate prices. Membership not required.

Limelight, 136 Shaftesbury Ave WC2. Two floors featuring modern dance rhythms. Good bar facilities. 2130–0300.

Ronnie Scott's, 47 Frith St. W1. The best jazz in London. Popularity makes advance enquiries essential.

Stringfellows, 16 Upper St. Martin's Lane WC2. Opulent decor; dance floor is of glass. Membership not essential but doorman checks would-be patrons.

The Gardens, 99 Kensington High St. W8. Roof-top club controlled by Richard Branson, owner of Virgin Records and Airline. Bar menu and luxury restaurant. Temporary membership arranged.

SHOPPING

Shops

Most shops are open Mon.–Sat. 0900–1730, with late evening opening to 1900 or 2000 on Wed. (Knightsbridge and Chelsea) or Thurs. (Oxford St., Bond St., Piccadilly, Kensington). Outside the central area shops close Wed. or Thurs. afternoon. A few in the West End close Sat. afternoon.

The following are the best-known shopping streets in Central London:

Bond St. W1 High-quality goods: fashions, jewellery, ceramics, paintings, cosmetics; Asprey for luxury gifts.

Charing Cross Rd WC2 New and second-hand books, musical instruments; Foyles, the booksellers, is at 119.

Covent Garden WC2 Wide variety of craft shops, with special market on Saturdays.

Edgware Rd W2 Hi-fi and electronics.

Jermyn St. W1 High-quality shirts, hats, *etc*, for men.

Kensington High St. W8 Major shopping centre with department stores, boutiques and hairdressers.

King's Rd, Chelsea Boutiques with fashionable and trendy clothes.

Knightsbridge SW1 Many luxurious shops, including Scotch House, the leading firm selling Scottish clothes, and Harrods, the department store which claims it can provide anything from a packet of pins to a live elephant.

Oxford St. W1 London's 'golden mile' has the leading department stores and the main shops of national chain stores supplying every kind of merchandise; Selfridges, Marks & Spencer, John Lewis, Debenhams.

Piccadilly W1 Simpsons, high-class department store; Fortnum & Mason, the finest purveyors of foods in London; bookshops.

Regent St. W1 Varied types of shops in prestige buildings, including Liberty's, the best-known source of textiles, carpets and imported household furnishings; Lillywhites, sports outfitters; Austin Reed, men's clothes.

Savile Row W1 Centre of the world's best – if expensive – men's suitings.

Tottenham Court Rd W1 Department stores devoted mainly to high-quality furniture and domestic goods; radio, TV and electronic equipment.

Markets

Street and under-cover markets offer a host of bargains and, with luck, some real treasures. Go as early as you can and do not be afraid to haggle over prices.

Camden Town, Antiques Market, Corner of High St. and Buck St. Thurs. 0700 onwards antiques; Fri. 0900–1700 arts and crafts; Sat. and Sun. 0900–1700 clothing.

Chelsea, Antiquarius, 135 King's Rd SW3. Covered antiques market Mon.–Sat. 1000–1800. Chenil Galleries, 181 King's Rd SW3. Covered antiques market Mon.–Sat. 1000–1800.

Covent Garden WC2, The Apple and Jubilee markets have the largest arts and crafts displays in Britain. Antiques Mon. 0600–1600; crafts, clothes, foods Tues.–Fri. 0900–1600; hand-made crafts Sat. & Sun. 0900–1700.

Earl's Court, Exhibition Centre market, Lillie Rd SW6. Antiques, clothes, bric-a-brac. Sun. 1000–1500.

East End, Petticoat Lane market, Middlesex St. E1. Clothes, general goods. Sun. 0800–1400. Adjacent is Designer Fashion market. Sun. 0700–1400.

Greenwich, Antiques market, High Rd SE10. Sat. (and Sun. in summer) 0800–1600.

Kensington, Fashion clothes market, High St. W8. Mon.–Sat. 1000–1800.

Mayfair, Antique Centre, 124 New Bond St. W1. Furniture and art. Weekdays 1000–1745. Gray's Mews Antique market, off Davies St. W1. Mon.–Fri. 1000–1800.

North Kensington, Portobello Rd market, W11. Stalls extending for more than 1 mi. Food, clothes Mon.–Sat.; flea market Fri. and Sat., antiques Sat. 0800 and through the day.

Southwark, New Caledonian market, Tower Bridge Rd SE1. New site for London's largest market. Now mainly antiques with dealers from all parts of the country. Fri. from dawn-1400.

Auction Rooms

Auctions are usually held five days a week, and hundreds of items are within the means of modest collectors. Even if you do not intend to buy, it is an experience to attend an auction to view valuable lots of every conceivable kind, from old masters and antique furniture to rare wines, silverware and porcelain.

The oldest is Sotheby's (founded 1744). Auctions are held at 34 New Bond St. W1, and 26 Conduit St. W1. Christie's (founded 1766) have premises at 8 King St., St James's, SW1, and 85 Old Brompton Rd, SW7. Other leading auctioneers are Bonhams, Montpelier St., Knightsbridge SW1, and 65 Lots Rd, Chelsea SW10; and Phillips, 7 Blenheim St., New Bond St. W1, 10 Salem Rd, Paddington W2, and Hayes Place, Marylebone NW1.

ENTERTAINMENT

Theatres

London is rightly regarded as the world's leading centre for live theatre. Current presentations are shown on posters at Underground stations. The *London Theatre Guide* (free) is obtainable at booking agencies and many hotels. *What's On* (weekly) from bookstalls and news-stands and the London newspapers list performance times, prices and phone numbers for credit card bookings. Most theatre seats are bookable either direct or through agencies (the latter charge a small commission).

The Leicester Square ticket booth (open 1200–1400 for matinees and

1430—1830 for evening performances) sells spare tickets at half price (plus a small service charge) on the day of the performance. Details of available seats at forty-five theatres in the scheme are displayed outside the booth. A similar facility is in the Theatre Museum, Russell St. WC2

Below are listed the West End theatres along with those a little more distant with a reputation for good plays. The type of play mentioned is only a guide to the usual policy of the house.

Adelphi, Strand WC2. Musicals.

Albery, St Martin's Lane WC2. Award-winning drama.

Aldwych, Aldwych WC2.

Ambassadors, West St. WC2.

Apollo, Shaftesbury Ave WC2.

Apollo Victoria, Wilton Rd SW1. Musicals.

Barbican, Barbican Centre EC2. Royal Shakespeare Company.

Barbican Pit, Barbican Centre EC2. Drama.

Cambridge, Earlham St. WC2. Drama.

Comedy, Panton St. WC2. Sophisticated plays.

Criterion, Piccadilly Circus. Usually comedy.

Donmar Warehouse, Earlham St. WC2. Repertory.

Drury Lane (Theatre Royal), Drury Lane WC2. Lavish musicals.

Duchess, Catherine St. WC2.

Duke of York's, St Martin's Lane WC2. Drama.

Fortune, Russell St. WC2. Small theatre for drama.

Garrick, Charing Cross Rd WC2. Comedy.

Globe, Shaftesbury Ave W1.

Haymarket (Theatre Royal), Haymarket SW1. Big-name plays.

Her Majesty's, Haymarket SW1.

Lyric, Shaftesbury Ave W1.

Lyric, King St. W6. Many classic revivals.

Mayfair, Stratton St. W1. Drama.

Mermaid, Blackfriars EC4. Unusual old and new plays (restaurant).

National Theatre, South Bank SE1. Olivier (open stage) prestige plays from repertory. Lyttelton (proscenium stage) important new plays and revivals of classics. Cottesloe (small: low prices) drama and comedy. Restaurant.

New London, Drury Lane WC2. Musicals.

Old Vic, Waterloo Rd SE1. Famous theatre, closed 1982. Restored and reopened 1983. Musicals and drama.

Open Air, Regent's Park NW1. Shakespeare, June–Sept.

Palace, Shaftesbury Ave W1. Musicals.

Palladium, Argyll St. W1. Top-line variety and musicals.

Phoenix, Charing Cross Rd WC2. Drama and sometimes films.

Piccadilly, Denman St. W1. Lavish musicals (restaurant).

Prince Edward, Old Compton St. W1 Musicals.

Prince of Wales, Coventry St. W1. Musicals.

Queen's, Shaftesbury Ave W1. Drama.

Royal Court, Sloane Sq. SW1. New plays.

St Martin's, West St. WC2. Current home of *The Mousetrap*, world's longest ever run: 32nd year in 1983.

Savoy, Strand WC2. Comedy or drama.

Shaftesbury, Shaftesbury Ave WC2. Comedy.

Strand, Aldwych WC2. Drama.

Stratford Theatre Royal, Angel Lane E15. East-end theatre with a high reputation for noteworthy new writers and plays.

Vaudeville, Strand WC2. Comedy.

Victoria Palace, Victoria St. SW1. Usually musicals.

Whitehall, Whitehall SW1. Varied types of play.

Wyndham's, Charing Cross Rd WC2. Drama

There are more than a hundred live theatres described as 'on the fringe' because of their somewhat unconventional policy or on account of their location beyond the area known as Theatreland. In some cases admission is to members only, but this is usually a formality for visitors for whom membership involves payment of a nominal fee on application shortly before visiting the theatre.

Information and tickets are available at the Fringe Box Office at the Criterion Theatre, Piccadilly Circus W1 (open Mon.–Thurs. 1000–1800, Fri. and Sat. 1000–1700). Below are a few examples of the better known establishments: Arts, Great Newport St. WC2; Café Theatre Studio, De Hems Public House, 88 Shaftesbury Ave W1; ICA, The Mall SW1; Lyric Studio, King St. W6; Theatre Upstairs, Sloane Sq. SW1; Young Vic, 66 The Cut SE1; Riverside Studios, Crisp Rd W6.

Opera and Ballet

The London Coliseum, St Martin's Lane WC2 presents opera in English. Periodically British and foreign ballet companies alternate with opera. With the aim of making opera available to all, special offers include low prices for one or two children accompanying two adults, reduced prices for students and senior citizens.

The Royal Opera House, Covent Garden WC2, is the home of the Royal

Opera company and the Royal Ballet; opera (in the original language) alternates with ballet. Although the magnificent auditorium seats 2000, demand for tickets is high and booking well in advance is always advisable. Some seats are reserved for sale on the day of the performance, but this usually requires each applicant (only one ticket per person) to arrive early in the day.

Sadler's Wells, Rosebery Ave EC1, is an excellent place to enjoy an evening (or matinee) of opera and ballet at bargain prices. This was the birthplace of the Royal Ballet under the inspiring direction of Ninette de Valois. Operas, operettas, and classical and modern ballet are adroitly mixed in the year-round presentations. As the theatre is off the usual tourist track (Underground Islington or buses 19, 38) it is worth writing in advance for the brochure-programme to Freepost, Sadler's Wells Foundation, Rosebery Ave, London EC1 B1A (no stamp required).

Concerts

Not a day passes without four or more musical events of international standard being presented in London's superb concert halls. On the South Bank the Royal Festival Hall, regarded acoustically as one of the best in the world, is used for orchestral and choral concerts and recitals by soloists of world-wide repute. Adjacent are the Purcell Room, offering chamber music, song recitals, and solo instrumentalists, and the rather larger Queen Elizabeth Hall, favoured by smaller orchestras. The Barbican Centre is the home of the London Symphony Orchestra and also features famous orchestras and artistes from abroad. The Royal Albert Hall, oldest of the concert halls (Kensington Gore SW7), usually presents popular classical music. Seats are less expensive than at other halls. This is the venue of the Promenade concerts, given nightly July–September, at which enthusiastic but penny-watching music lovers can stand in the well of the building, closer to the performers than the thousand or so in the seating above them.

Other halls are St John's, Smith Sq. SW1, with lunchtime and evening concerts most weekdays; the Wigmore Hall, 36 Wigmore St. W1, noted for chamber music and soloists.

London is also unique in the number and variety of recitals in its churches at lunchtime on weekdays. This refers particularly to the City churches. They are too numerous to mention, but on a visit to the City the notice board outside the church gives the details. These concerts, lasting an hour or less, are popular with City office workers. Admission is at a nominal cost or voluntary donation.

Band concerts, costing nothing to enjoy, are held during the summer in the Embankment Gardens, Charing Cross (lunchtime and early evening), Lincoln's Inn Fields (lunchtime Tues. and Thurs.), Hyde Park, St James's Park, and Regent's Park (days and times vary).

Cinemas

London's cinemas usually open at about 1400 weekdays and on Sun. about 1515, with a late show on Fri. and Sat. at about 2300. Many offer reduced prices all day Mon. and matinees Tues.–Fri. Films are authorised for exhibition under certificates: U: suitable for all ages; PG: parental guidance (some scenes unsuitable for children); AA/15: no one under 15 admitted; X/18: no one under 18 admitted.

First-run cinemas in the West End and Central areas: Warner, Leicester Sq. WC2 (4 screens) Odeons in Haymarket SW1, Leicester Sq. WC2. Marble Arch W1; Leicester Square theatre WC2; Empire, Leicester Sq. WC2 (3 screens), Plaza, Lower Regent St. SW1 (4 screens). The numerous Cannon theatres, mostly with first-run and pre-general release films, include those in Marylebone Rd NW1; Haymarket SW1; Oxford St. W1; Panton St. SW1; Piccadilly W1; Charing Cross Rd WC2; Shaftesbury Ave W1 (2 screens); Tottenham Court Rd W1 (3 screens).

Cultural and foreign language films are screened at the Curzon cinemas in Curzon St. W1; Shaftesbury Ave W1; Charing Cross Rd WC2; Lumière, St Martin's Lane, WC2; Chelsea, King's Rd SW3; Minema, 45 Knightsbridge SW1; Renoir, Brunswick Sq. WC1 (2 screens); Première, Swiss Centre, Leicester Sq. WC2 (3 screens).

The ICA Centre, Nash House, the Mall, SW1 (4 screens) features cultural films and discussions; daily membership available for 60p. The National Film theatre, under south end of Waterloo Bridge is run by the National Film Institute and shows notable artistic and popular films of the past and present; weekly membership available for 70p.

Free film presentations are screened at Canada House, Trafalgar Sq. WC2, usually Wed. and Fri. evenings (Canadian films); Imperial War Museum, Lambeth Rd SE1, Sat. and Sun. afternoons (documentary and fictional war films); Tate Gallery, Millbank SW1, usually daily at 1100 and 1430 (films concerned with the arts). London's local newspapers publish full details of programmes, times, and tel. nos.

SPORTS
AND ACTIVITIES

Athletics The main centre for athletic meetings is Crystal Palace National Sports Centre SE19. Information about events can be obtained from the British Amateur Athletics Board, Francis House, Francis St. SW1. The annual Marathon race on a Sunday (April or May) starts in Greenwich Park and finishes on Constitution Hill near Buckingham Palace. Training and team events are features of the Michael Sobell Sports Centre, Hornsey Rd N7.

Boating Boats may be rented on the Serpentine in Hyde Park and on the lakes in Battersea Park and Regent's Park, and on the Thames upriver from Putney.

Brass rubbing Facsimiles of medieval and Tudor brasses from cathedrals and churches all over England have been assembled in the cloisters of Westminster Abbey and in St Margaret's beside it, in Westminster, as a fund-raising scheme for both Abbey and church. Other centres at St James's church, Piccadilly W1 (week days 1000—1800, Sun. 1200—1800, advice and materials available), and All Hallows-by-the-Tower, Byward St. EC3 (Mon.—Fri. 0930—1800, Sat. and Sun. 1000—1800).

Cricket Both Lord's, St John's Wood NW8, home of the Middlesex Cricket Club, and the Oval, Kennington SE11, home of the Surrey Cricket Club, have matches most weekdays in summer.

Fishing The Thames above Richmond provides good angling. The reservoir at Walthamstow E4 is open for fishing mid-June to mid-March. A water-rod licence has to be obtained from the Thames Water Authority, New River Head, Rosebery Avenue EC1R 4TP.

Football Association football grounds are at Highbury N5 (Arsenal); The Valley SE7 (Charlton); Stamford Bridge SW6 (Chelsea); Selhurst Park SE25 (Crystal Palace); the Den SE14 (Millwall); Brisbane Rd E10 (Orient); Loftus Rd W12 (Fulham Park); White Hart Lane N17 (Tottenham Hotspur); Upton Park E13 (West Ham).

Golf Public courses can be found at Mitcham Common, Surrey; Richmond Park; Chingford E4, Wimbledon Common.

Greyhound racing There are six courses in the London area. All have restaurants. Catford Stadium, Catford Bridge SE6 (Thurs. and Sat. from 1945). Hackney Stadium, Weterden Rd E15 (Tues. and Thurs. from 1400). Harringay Stadium, Green Lanes N4 (Mon. and Fri. from 1945). Walthamstow Stadium, Chingford E4 (Tues. and Sat. from 1945). Wembley Stadium, Empire Way, Wembley, Middlesex (Mon. and Fri. from 1945). Wimbledon Stadium, Plough Lane SW17 (Wed. and Fri. from 1945).

Horse racing Courses near London are Ascot, Berkshire; Epsom, Surrey; Kempton Park, Surrey; Sandown Park, Surrey; Windsor, Berkshire.

Horse riding Mounts may be rented in Dulwich Park SE21; Hampstead Heath NW3; Hyde Park SW1; Richmond Park, Surrey; Wimbledon Common SW19.

Ice hockey and ice skating The main rinks are Queen's Club, Queensway W2; Richmond ice rink, Twickenham, Middlesex; Streatham Ice Rink SW16; Empire Pool, Wembley.

Rugby The principal grounds for rugby union football are at Twickenham, Richmond, Blackheath and Roehampton.

Swimming All local authorities maintain swimming pools. In Central London: Marshall St. Centre W1; Porchester Centre W2; Chelsea Sports Centre, Manor St. SW3; Kensington New Pools, Walmer Rd W11; Oasis, 32 Endell St. WC2, Crystal Palace National Sports Centre, Norwood SE19 (Olympic size pool). The following pools are open air in summer. Hyde Park Lido; Parliament Hill Lido NW5; Hampstead Ponds, NW3.

Tennis Most of London's parks have hard courts for public use. For spectators the major tournaments are held at Wimbledon SW19 (where the lawn tennis championships are held the last week of June and the first week of July); Queen's Club, West Kensington W8; and at Hurlingham Park SW6. Indoor championships are held at Wembley Arena.

YOUNG LONDON

Where to Stay

For anyone arriving without making previous arrangements, the best course is to go to the Tourist Information Centre at Victoria railway station SW1, which runs a budget accommodation service for short or long stays in hostels, dormitories and boarding houses.

There will be a better choice of accommodation if you write to the London Visitor and Convention Bureau, 26 Grosvenor Gardens SW1W 0DU at least six weeks in advance, giving your price-range for a room. Make sure that you enclose return postage or international reply coupon.

1 *Wembley Stadium*
2 *The Oval cricket ground*
3 *Portobello Road*
4 *The Lord Mayor's Show*
5 *Boutique, King's Road*
6 *Royal Horse Artillery, Hyde Park*
7 *Elton John, Tussaud's*
8 *In the Tower of London*
9 *Camden Lock*
10 *Elephant house, London Zoo*

Members of the Youth Hostels Association, or its affiliated organizations overseas, can obtain details of hostels in and around London either from HQ at Trevelyan House, St Albans, Hertfordshire, or the London Office, 29 John Adam St., Strand WC2. Youth hostels in London itself are heavily booked. The best one is in the grounds of the Commonwealth Institute, Holland Park W11, built as a memorial to King George VI, and incorporating part of a 17th-century mansion. Other hostels are at 38 Bolton Gardens SW5, a quiet road running parallel to Old Brompton Rd, near Earl's Court; 84 Highgate West Hill, Highgate N6, alongside Parliament Hill with its bathing pool and ponds and the cemetery famous as the burial place of Karl Marx; 36 Carter Lane EC4 (closed Dec.–mid-March), off Ludgate Hill, near St Paul's.

Youth hostels which offer the possibility of a base in rural England with day trips to London are: Henley-on-Thames, Oxfordshire (56km/35mi); Ivinghoe, Buckinghamshire(53km/33mi); Jordans, Buckinghamshire (43km/27mi); St Albans, Hertfordshire (34km/21mi); Windsor, Berkshire (37km/23mi). They are all within about one and a half hours of central London by car or train.

Both the YMCA and YWCA maintain clubs with sleeping accommodation in London. The YMCA in Great Russell St. WC1, between Tottenham Court Rd and the British Museum, has 764 bedrooms, and recreation and sports facilities; the YWCA's central club, with comparable facilities, is a little further east along Great Russell St. In Fitzroy Sq. WC1, east of Great Portland St. at the Euston Rd end, is the YMCA Indian Students Union building and hostel.

Overseas students on vacation will find advice on accommodation and matters of interest at the International Students' House, Park Crescent, Portland Place W1. The building is marked by a bust of President Kennedy at the front.

Pitching a tent, spending the night in a sleeping bag or merely sleeping rough is not permitted in London parks or in any urban open space. Hackney Marsh site, Millfields Rd E5, is an extensive International camping site. For other camping places within easy reach of the capital, consult the magazine *Caravan*. Membership of the Camping Club of Great Britain gives special facilities. Details from 11 Grosvenor Place SW1.

Food

Self-service cafés and restaurants are always the cheapest and, apart from a restriction in some places about occupying a table from 1200 to 1400 while having only a cup of coffee, no one minds how little you buy or how long you take to eat it. The small, independently run places, where sandwiches are freshly prepared behind the counter, are best for quality and quantity. There are a good many pizza houses and hamburger joints. Quality varies but at least you can see the food before you buy.

Take-away restaurants and cafés are numerous, particularly for Chinese and Indian foods, and American-style roast chicken. The attraction is that by law food consumed on the premises carries Value Added Tax (VAT is a variable tax, shown separately on a bill for services, but included in the purchase price of goods) while food taken away does not. This means that by eating away from a place you save about 15 percent. Britain's famous fish and chip shops are also mainly take-away, and offer a cheap, nutritious and appetizing meal. It is quite usual, by the way, for the impecunious to buy just the chips. Blooms, 90 Whitechapel High St. E1, sells kosher food to take away. And Soho has some kosher nosh-bars in Great Windmill St. and Berwick St.

As hygiene standards vary in the mobile vans found in side streets in the evening, serving hot dogs and hamburgers, they are best avoided by the cautious. This stricture does not apply to the decreasing number of so-called coffee stalls which for a century and more have catered for shift-workers and insomniacs right through the night, with meat pies, sandwiches, mugs of strong tea and, comparatively rarely, coffee. (For information about London's pubs, see pp. 15, 16–17.)

Shopping

Today's 'in' clothes are on display in virtually every large store in the West End, Kensington and Knightsbridge, and most of them run a separate section for the under-25s. Generally regarded as among the best are Miss Selfridge (separate entrance from the main store, in Duke St.), Harrods in Knightsbridge, and C & A, at the Marble Arch end of Oxford St. Tomorrow's styles start in boutiques, mostly in the King's Rd and its offshoots in Chelsea; Kensington High St.; and Covent Garden.

Entertainment

Concert halls and theatres are listed in the newspapers. The National Theatre complex on South Bank encourages students (identification of status needed) to attend afternoon performances at reduced prices, usually a flat rate for any seat. More than 50 percent of theatres offer reduced prices to students for vacant seats just before the performance.

The Shaw Theatre, 100 Euston Rd NW1, admits young people under 21 and students to all performances at half price. The Young Vic, The Cut SE1, and the Theatre Upstairs, Royal Court Theatre, Sloane Sq. SW1, feature plays to appeal to a young audience with modestly priced seats. The fringe theatres which have sprung up in the Tottenham Court Rd and Covent Garden districts present plays by new authors with new actors, and are inexpensive. Often run on a shoestring, they cannot advertise widely. See posters or enquire at Fringe Box Office, Criterion Theatre, Piccadilly Circus.

Cinema seats in the West End are fairly expensive and there are no concessions for students or young adults, but cinemas in the inner suburbs are much cheaper, and may be showing the same films. Foreign and artistic films are shown at the Everyman, Hampstead NW3; the Gate, Notting Hill Gate W11; the Classic cinema, Victoria St. SW1, among others.

Discotheques, large and small, flourish in Chelsea, Kensington, Charing Cross Rd and Soho. The easiest way to find out the most popular discos is to buy a copy of *What's On* or *Time Out*.

Folk and Country, Reggae, Soul and Jazz concerts are innumerable every night (see *Time Out* weekly guide for details). Most famous jazz club is Ronnie Scott's, 47 Frith St. W1. Mon.—Sat. 2030—0300 (membership fee).

Live shows by pop stars and groups are well advertised. The major shows are presented at Earl's Court, Wembley or the Albert Hall. In Battersea Park folk, country and jazz music concerts are presented most Sat. and Sun. evenings in the summer. Jazz concerts are held at Holland Park W11, once a week in June and July.

If you want to enjoy active sport, the National Sports and Recreation Centre, Crystal Palace SE19, has facilities for athletics, team games and swimming.

CHILDREN'S LONDON

What's On

There is a special phone number (246 8007) you can dial to find out the various daily events for children. Kidsline (222 8070) also has information on children's activities (0900—1600 weekdays).

Getting Around

If you are under 16, London's buses and trains are a cheap way of seeing the sights of London. You pay a flat rate for your ticket no matter how far you travel on any one bus. You can save even more with a London Explorer Pass which gives you unlimited travel on bus or the underground. You can buy it for 1, 3, 4 or 7 days. The pass also includes discount vouchers for fees to enter London's best-known attractions. The Travelcard also gives you the same unlimited travel, but only after 0930 Mon.—Fri. and all day Sat. and Sun. These special offers apply to anyone under 16, but 14 and 15 year olds must carry a child rate photocard.

Things to See

Most of the buildings and places in the Gazetteer (pp. 77—124) will interest children as much as adults. Below are some of the museums of special interest (addresses in alphabetical list of museums and galleries pp. 47—57).
Bethnal Green Museum of Childhood The toys and games your great-grandparents used to have. **Geological Museum** Free film shows about the land on which we live. **Horniman Museum** All sorts of ideas for leisure activities when you get home. And you can borrow drawing materials if you wish. **London Toy and Model Museum** Lavish displays of toys and models, including working trains and cars. **Museum of Mankind** Free film shows about our ancestors. **National Maritime Museum** Apart from the wonderful models of ships down the ages, there is a Planetarium to show the movement of the stars and planets. Afterwards you can board a famous sailing clipper, *Cutty Sark*. **Natural History Museum** If you like birds and animals you can spend days here. If you haven't much time the best part is the Hall of Human Biology where you can play constructive games and watch shows about how your body works. **Pollock's Toy Museum** A tiny place with all sorts of toys from the past, including toy theatres. Most days there is a Punch and Judy show, and lucky visitors get a gingerbread man when they leave. **Postal Museum** If you collect stamps this is a place to make you envious, as there are many thousands of rare stamps covering every year from 1878 and some 200 countries. Nearby is the main London Post Office, a good place to buy the special sets of stamps being issued in Britain. **RAF Museum** Three museums in one – for the RAF, Battle of Britain, and Bomber Command. Real aircraft to inspect. There is a free cinema showing exciting films of aircraft in

action. **Science Museum** Almost everything here will fascinate you, and there is a special children's gallery with models of machines which spring to life when you press the button. **Tussaud's** If you have ever wondered what the people in history books, or the famous of today, from pop stars to politicians, look like, you can see them here in lifelike wax effigies. There is also the Chamber of Horrors to test your nerves. Next door is a Planetarium, with the whole of the solar system moving before your eyes while the wonder of it is explained in a commentary. **Victoria and Albert Museum** The attendants here will help you if you want to draw any of the exhibits of beautiful things that help to make a house into a home.

Out of Doors

In Battersea Park there is a good section for young children, with a sandpit, paddling pool and adventure playground. On Hampstead Heath, right at the top of the hill, is the Leg of Mutton Pond for sailing model boats, and on the slopes clear of trees you can watch – or take part in – kite and model aircraft flying. A little farther east is Parliament Hill Fields Lido with special facilities for children, even if they cannot swim. Hyde Park Lido on the Serpentine is larger, but well looked after by lifeguards; you can paddle at the edge or just sunbathe and play on the grass alongside the water. The playground in Kensington Gardens was the gift of an author who loved children, J. M. Barrie, and the statue of Peter Pan is just beside the water. In Regent's Park there is a shallow pool with motorboats which children can operate themselves, as well as paddleboats worked by rotating handles. And, of course, in the corner of the park is the Zoo with its animals, birds, reptiles and insects; rides on elephants, camels and llamas; plus a children's zoo. Lastly, Wimbledon Common possesses three fine lakes, and is popular with model boat enthusiasts and picnickers. The common also has a windmill built in 1817 and, in the south-west corner, Caesar's Camp and Well built, according to legend, by Julius Caesar.

Entertainment

The Little Angel Marionette Theatre, 14 Dagmar Passage, Cross St. N1 gives shows Sat. and Sun. at 1100. Booking advisable by phone (226 1787). The Unicorn Theatre, 6 Great Newport St. WC2 (part of the Arts Theatre Club) is a theatre for children, with puppet shows Sat. and Sun. 1430. The Polka Children's Theatre, 240 The Broadway, Wimbledon SW19, presents puppets and mime shows morning and afternoon between 1000–1600 Tues.–Fri., 1200–1830 Sat. There

is also a museum of puppets and toys, and a children's café.

Shops

The biggest toy shop in Britain – four floors with every kind of toy – is Hamleys in Regent St. Both Selfridges and Harrods have splendid toy departments, and specialist toy shops are the Owl and the Pussy Cat, Flask Walk, Hampstead NW3, and Abbat's shop at 74 Wigmore St. W1. If you like books visit the Children's Book Centre, Church St., Kensington W8, and you may even manage to get the autograph of a writer who is also visiting the shop. Foyles, Charing Cross Rd WC2, and Harrods also have fine children's book departments.

GENERAL INFORMATION

Chemists (pharmacies) with a dispensing section for medicines open during normal shopping hours (0900–1730), usually with one late night opening shown on a door notice. Boots, in Piccadilly Circus, is open weekdays 0900–1900. Bliss Chemists, 50 Willesden Lane NW6 is open 24 hours a day.

Electricity Current is generated at 230–250 V 50 cycles AC. Light sockets and power points are for the bayonet type of plug. Overseas visitors may require an adaptor, and some electrical items with motors may not be operable due to the difference in frequency of the cycles.

Health Any visitor to Britain may consult a doctor in the National Health Service but will normally have to pay for it, including the cost of any drugs, medicines and hospital treatment. The charges do not, however, apply to persons who have been in the United Kingdom for 12 months, have come to work or settle, are spouses or children of persons settled in the UK, or belong to an EEC country or one which has a reciprocal arrangement. All visitors should take out health insurance before travelling, or immediately on arrival.

In case of emergency, hospitals with casualty departments open 24 hours a day in Central London are: Middlesex, Mortimer St. W1; New Charing Cross, Fulham Palace Rd W6; St Bartholomew's Smithfield EC1; St Mary's, Praed St. W2; University College, Gower St. WC1; Moorfields Eye Hospital, High Holborn WC1.

Rabies It cannot be too strongly stressed that the UK totally prohibits the importation of live (or dead) animals from the rest of the world except under licence. One of the conditions of the licence is that

Duty-free allowances *subject to change*		Bought duty free or outside EEC	Duty and tax paid in EEC
Tobacco	Cigarettes	200	300
	or		
	Cigars *small*	100	150
	or		
	Cigars *large*	50	75
	or		
	Pipe tobacco	250 gm	400 gm
Alcohol	Spirits *over 38.8° proof*	1 litre	1½ litres
	or		
	Fortified or sparkling wine	2 litres	3 litres
	plus		
	Table wine	2 litres	5 litres
Perfume		50 gm	75 gm
Toilet water		250 cc	375 cc
Other goods		£28	£163

(Note in box at left: "Double if you live outside Europe")

US customs permit duty free $300 retail value
of purchases per person, 1 quart of liquor per person over 21,
and 100 cigars per person.

Customs

The table above summarizes the duty- and tax-free allowances which visitors may bring into the country. (People under the age of 17 are not entitled to tobacco and drinks allowance.)

Prohibited goods include controlled drugs, firearms and explosives (including fireworks) flick knives, horror comics and indecent or obscene literature and films, radio transmitters operating on certain frequencies (*eg* walkie-talkies and CB radios); meat not fully cooked; most plants, bulbs, trees and certain fruits and vegetables; most animals and birds alive or dead, and certain articles made from fur or skin of rare species of animals and reptiles. (For information on rabies, see p. 26.)

On leaving the United Kingdom some goods are subject to export control. This applies particularly to antiques and works of art more than 50 years old and valued at £8000 or more. Further information obtainable from HM Customs and Excise, Kent House, Upper Ground, London SE1 9PS (tel. 928 0533). (The foregoing regulations are liable to change.)

Currency and Banks

The pound (£) consists of 100 pence. Coins are 1p, 2p, 5p, 10p, 20p, 50p, and £1. Notes are issued in £5, £10, £20 and £50 denominations.

Banks open 0930–1530 (1500 in the City) Mon.–Fri. Some branches also open 1630–1800 Thurs. and 1000–1200 Sats. (See also Public Holidays, p. 28.) All banks provide facilities for the exchange of traveller's checks and foreign currency (take your passport). Banks offer the most favourable rates of exchange. Numerous exchange bureaus, with the same opening hours as shops (see p. 17), frequently quote a slightly less favourable rate. Hotels, restaurants and shops, when accepting traveller's checks, usually charge commission above that of a bank charge.

Credit cards issued by international organizations are valid in larger shops and good-class restaurants.

animals are kept in approved quarantine premises for as long as six months in most cases (including domestic pets). No exemptions are allowed in respect of animals which have been vaccinated against rabies. Penalties for smuggling any creature involve imprisonment, unlimited fines and, in certain circumstances, destruction of the animal.

For details of animal importation and quarantine regulations apply to Ministry of Agriculture (Animal Health Division), Hook Rise South, Tolworth, Surbiton, Surrey KT6 7NF.

Lost property On British Rail trains and stations: lost property office at London main-line terminal of Rail Region concerned. On London Transport buses and Underground: 200 Baker St. NW1. On Green Line Coaches: nearest London Country Bus Services garage. In taxis: 15 Penton St. N1 (nearest Underground: Angel). In street or park: call in at any police station.

Police stations in the City and Central London: 26 Old Jewry EC2 (City of London Police); New Scotland Yard, Broadway SW1; 2 Lucas Pl. SW3; 70 Theobalds Rd WC1; Hyde Park W2 (north of Serpentine); 72 Earl's Court Rd W8; 1 Seymour St. W1; 63 Rochester Row SW1; 56 Tottenham Court Rd W1; 10 Vine St. W1; 27 Savile Row W1.

Postal services Most post offices are open from 0900–1730 Mon.–Fri. and 0830–1200 Sat. Postage stamps are sold only at post offices or sub-post offices, the latter in a section of a shop. Rates for air mail letters to addresses outside Europe are charged according to three zones, with a maximum weight of 10g for the lowest rate. It is advisable to have the post office clerk weigh the letter on his special scales and not to rely on the packet scales placed for use by the public. Overseas parcel postage rates vary according to destination. Normally a parcel must not be sealed but secured with string which can be untied. A customs declaration has to be filled in.

Principal **post offices** in the City and Central London: King Edward St. EC1 (London Chief Office); 111 Baker St. W1; 15 Broadwick St. W1; 78 Chancery Lane WC2; 232 King's Rd SW3; 165 Euston Rd NW1; 7 Great Portland St. W1; 257 Kensington High St. W8; 55 Knightsbridge SW1; 28 Marylebone High St. W1; 22 Queen St. W1; 44 Parliament St. SW1; 11 Regent St. SW1; 9 King's Rd SW1; 71 Southampton Row WC1; 87 St James's St. SW1; 24 William IV St. (off Trafalgar Sq.) WC2 (0800–2000 Mon.–Fri.; 1000–1700 Sat.); 110 Victoria St. SW1.

Public holidays New Year's Day, Easter Monday, Mayday (first Mon. in May), spring holiday (usually last Mon. in May), late summer holiday (usually last Mon. in August), Boxing Day (26 Dec.). Banks are closed on these days, and also on Good Friday and Christmas Day. Most museums and art galleries are closed on New Year's Day, Good Friday, Christmas Day and Boxing Day.

Telephones Phone booths are to be found in post offices and on the street in busy areas; pay boxes take 5p and 10p coins. All inland calls from London can be dialled without the help of an operator. For calls outside the London area a town or area code of two, three or four figures has to be dialled before the actual number. These code numbers are displayed in the telephone booth or in the booklet of dialling instructions issued with the telephone directory. This booklet also contains the codes of overseas countries, the majority of which can be dialled direct.

International calls are cheaper between 2000 and 0600 and all day Sat. and Sun. Coin boxes (pay phones) can be used only for calls to Europe and North Africa.

For any call, inland or overseas, the operator may be contacted for assistance by dialling 100.

For emergency calls for police, fire or ambulance dial 999 and state the service you require. Do not insert any coins.

There is no inland telegram service in Britain. Overseas messages can be dictated by phone (dial 100 and ask for Telemessage). They will be transmitted by phone and normally delivered next day.

A selection of the main events of the day in London and district is obtainable by

Mosque, Regent's Park

dialling: 246 8041 (in English); 246 8043 (in French); 246 8045 (in German); 246 8049 (in Italian); 246 8047 (in Spanish); 246 8007 has recorded information on events of special appeal to children. The weather forecast for the London area is obtainable on 246 8091. Information about road conditions within 80km 50mi of London is on 246 8021.

Useful publications *In Britain*, an English Tourist Board magazine, contains details of current entertainments in London and the rest of the country as well as topical articles and a diary of the year's notable events. *What's On and Where to Go*, *Time Out* and *City Limits* are published weekly and provide information on theatres, cinemas, concerts, art exhibitions, sports events as well as listing restaurants and night spots. All the above publications are available from newsagents and street vendors.

Disabled visitors Many museums, theatres and restaurants provide aid for the disabled. A guide, *London for the Disabled*, with details of recommended hotels, is available from the Central Council for the Disabled, 25 Mortimer St. W1.

USEFUL ADDRESSES

Aliens Registration Office (for those staying in Britain for more than three months), 10 Lamb's Conduit St., Theobalds Rd WC1.
American Club, 95 Piccadilly W1.
American Express, 6 Haymarket SW1.
British Rail Travel Centre, 12 Lower Regent St. SW1.
City of London Information Centre, St Paul's Churchyard EC4.
English Speaking Union, 37 Charles St. W1.
Tourist Information Service (London and English regions); Victoria Station (730 3488). Mon.—Sat. 0900—1800 for phone; personal callers daily 0900—2030.
London Tourist Information Centres also at Heathrow Terminals 1, 2 and 3; Selfridges (ground floor) Oxford St. W1; Harrods Knightsbridge SW1; Richmond Library, Little Green, Richmond; Tourist Centre, 22 High St. Uxbridge.
London Transport Enquiry Offices; Piccadilly Circus, Oxford Circus, Heathrow Central, King's Cross, Euston, Victoria, Charing Cross and St James's Park Underground stations; British Rail Travel Centre, 12 Lower Regent St.
National Express Coaches Enquiry Bureau, Victoria Coach Station, Buckingham Palace Rd SW1.
Green Line Coaches, Eccleston Bridge, Victoria SW1.

Embassies, Consulates and Commonwealth Offices

Australia Australia House, Strand WC2. **Austria** 18 Belgrave Mews West SW1. **Bangladesh** 28 Queen's Gate SW7. **Belgium** 103 Eaton Sq. SW1. **Canada** Canada House, Trafalgar Sq. SW1. **Denmark** 55 Sloane St. SW1. **Eire** 17 Grosvenor Place SW1. **France** 24 Rutland Gate SW7. **Greece** 1a Holland Park W11. **India** India House, Aldwych WC2. **Italy** Three Kings' Yard, Davies St. W1. **Netherlands** 38 Hyde Park Gate SW7. **New Zealand** New Zealand House, Haymarket SW1. **Norway** 25 Belgrave Sq. SW1. **Pakistan** 35 Lowndes Sq. SW1. **Portugal** 11 Belgrave Sq. SW1. **South Africa** South Africa House, Trafalgar Sq. WC2. **Spain** 20 Draycott Pl. SW3. **Sri Lanka** 13 Hyde Park Gardens W2. **Sweden** 11 Montagu Place W1. **Switzerland** 16 Montagu Place W1. **United States of America** 1 Grosvenor Sq. W1. **West Germany** 23 Belgrave Sq. SW1.

Churches

The principal **Church of England** (Anglican) churches in Central London are: St Paul's Cathedral, EC4; Westminster Abbey, SW1; Southwark Cathedral, SE1; St George's, Hanover Sq. W1; St James's, Piccadilly W1; St Margaret's SW1; St Martin-in-the-Fields, Trafalgar Sq. WC2; St Marylebone NW1; St Paul's, Covent Garden WC2. **Roman Catholic:** Westminster Cathedral, Ashley Place, Victoria St. SW1; Brompton Oratory, Brompton Rd SW7; Church of the Immaculate Conception, Farm St., Berkeley Sq. W1; St. James's, Spanish Place W1; Notre Dame, Leicester Place WC2. **Christian Science:** Sloane Terrace, SW1; Curzon St. W1; **Church of Scotland:** St Columba's, Pont St. SW1. **United Reformed:** City Temple, Holborn Viaduct EC1. **Greek Orthodox:** 184 Mare St. E8; Godolphin Rd W12; 5 Craven Hill W2; Golders Green Rd NW11. **Islam:** The Mosque, Regent's Park NW1. **Jewish:** West London Synagogue, 34 Upper Berkeley St. W1; Central Synagogue, Great Portland St. W1. **Methodist:** Central Hall, Westminster SW1; Wesley's Chapel, City Rd EC1. **Presbyterian:** Regent Sq. WC1; St John's, Allen St. W8. **Russian Orthodox Church in Exile:** Emperor's Gate SW7. **Society of Friends:** (Quakers): Friends House, Euston Rd NW1; Meeting House, St Martin's Lane WC2. **Unitarian:** Essex Church, Palace Gardens Terrace W8.

ANNUAL EVENTS

To avoid disappointment check precise dates and details with London Visitor and Convention Bureau Mon.—Sat. 0900—1800 (tel. 730 3488).

January
Soon after Christmas the London shops hold their January sales which can yield fantastic bargains. International Boat Show, Earl's Court, Warwick Rd SW5 (early Jan.). Chinese New Year festivities, Gerrard St., Soho W1 (Jan. or Feb.).

February
Cruft's Dog Show, Earl's Court; Scouts and Guides Founder's Day service, Westminster Abbey (22 Feb); Folk Music Festival, Royal Albert Hall; Hobbies Fair, Earl's Court SW5.

March
Distribution of oranges to children at St Clement Danes, Strand (date varies). Antiques Fair, Chelsea Old Town Hall, King's Rd SW3 (mid-month). Country music festival, Wembley Arena (last week). Ideal Home Exhibition, Earl's Court.

March or April
Oxford and Cambridge boat race on Thames, Putney to Mortlake (usually Sat. before Easter week). Easter Parade, Battersea Park SW11 (Easter Sun.). Fair, Hampstead Heath NW3 (Easter Mon.). Harness Horse Parade, Regent's Park NW1 (Easter Mon.).

April
London Fashion Exhibition, Earl's Court Warwick Rd SW5. Primrose Day: decoration of statue of Disraeli, Parliament Sq. SW1 (19 Apr.). Birthday of the Queen: gun salutes from Hyde Pk and the Tower (21 Apr.). Shakespeare's birthday service, Southwark Cathedral (23 Apr.). Anzac Day: memorial service, Westminster Abbey (25 Apr.). London Marathon (Sun. in April or early May). Camden Arts Festival of Dance, Music, Opera, and Jazz.

May
Opening of Royal Academy Summer Art Exhibition, Burlington House, Piccadilly W1. Association Football cup final, Wembley (usually second Sat.). Rugby League Challenge Cup Final at Wembley (mid-May). Flower show, Royal Hospital Grounds, Chelsea, SW3 (usually in last week). Commonwealth Day: ceremonies at Cenotaph, Whitehall; Unknown Warrior's tomb, Westminster Abbey; and Lincoln statue, Parliament Sq. (24 May).

Trooping the Colour

June

Trooping the Colour ceremony, Horse Guards Parade (Sat. nearest 11 June to mark Queen's official birthday). Race meeting, including the Derby and Oaks, Epsom, Surrey (usually first week). Royal Ascot race meeting, Ascot, Berkshire (usually third week). Lawn Tennis championships, Church Rd, Wimbledon SW19 (last week in June, first week in July). Festival of Sport, Brockwell Park, Lambeth SE24.

July

Henry Wood promenade concerts of classical music, Albert Hall (till Sept.). Royal Tournament, Earl's Court, Warwick Rd SW5; athletic championships, White City (mid-month). Royal International Horse Show, Wembley Arena (usually last week). City of London Festival in alternate years, 1988, 1990, *etc.* (last days).

August

International sports festival, Crystal Palace (usually mid-month). West Indian Carnival, Notting Hill (Bank Holiday weekend). Clipper Week river festival on Thames at Greenwich.

September

Battle of Britain Day: fly-past over London by RAF (15 Sept.). Autumn antiques fair, Chelsea Old Town Hall, King's Rd, SW3 (last two weeks).

October

Opening of Royal Courts of Justice with judges in State robes attending Westminster Abbey service, followed by procession to House of Lords (1 Oct. or first Mon.). Horse of the Year Show, Wembley Arena (first week). Trafalgar Day: service and parade, Nelson's column, Trafalgar Sq. (21 Oct). State Opening of Parliament (Oct./Nov.).

November

Start of veteran car run to Brighton, at Hyde Pk Corner (usually first Sun.). Guy Fawkes' Day: firework displays in many areas (5 Nov.). State opening of Parliament by the Queen (usually in first week). Armistice Day: Festival of Remembrance, Albert Hall (11 Nov.). Remembrance Day ceremony attended by the Queen, members of the royal family, statesmen, leaders of the armed services, and representatives of foreign countries, Cenotaph, Whitehall (Sun. nearest 11 Nov.). Lord Mayor's Procession and Show through the streets of the City of London from Guildhall to the Law Courts (Sat. nearest 12 Nov.). London film festival, National Film Theatre, South Bank (into Dec.).

December

Westminster carol services (20–28 Dec.). Watch Night gathering of exiled Scots on steps of St Paul's (31 Dec.). Exhibition of camping and travel, Olympia (Dec.-Jan.).

Lord Mayor's Coach and Pikemen

London's Underground

Jubilee Line underground train

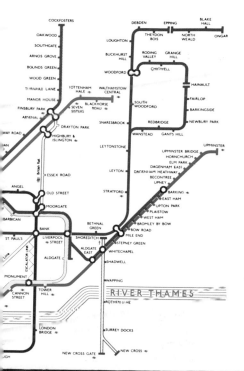

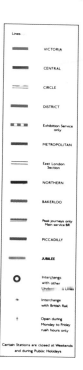

Lines	
	VICTORIA
	CENTRAL
	CIRCLE
	DISTRICT
	Exhibition Service only
	METROPOLITAN
	East London Section
	NORTHERN
	BAKERLOO
	Peak journeys only Main service BR
	PICCADILLY
	JUBILEE
○	Interchange with other Underground Links
⊕	Interchange with British Rail
†	Open during Monday to Friday rush hours only

Certain Stations are closed at Weekends and during Public Holidays

London Underground sign

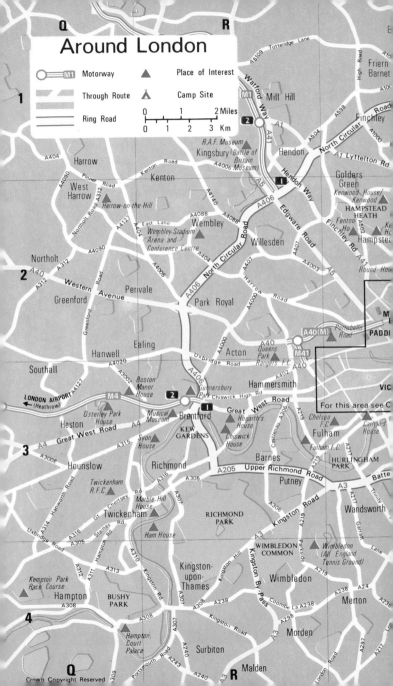

Central London Maps

The maps of London are based upon
Ordnance Survey maps with the sanction of
the Controller of Her Majesty's Stationery
Office. Crown Copyright reserved.

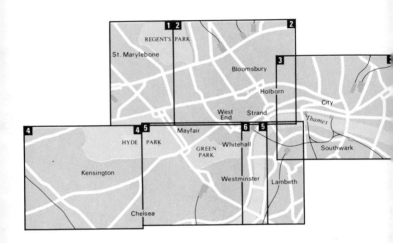

Key to Symbols

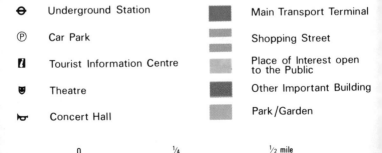

⊖	Underground Station	Main Transport Terminal
℗	Car Park	Shopping Street
🛈	Tourist Information Centre	Place of Interest open to the Public
🎭	Theatre	Other Important Building
🎵	Concert Hall	Park/Garden

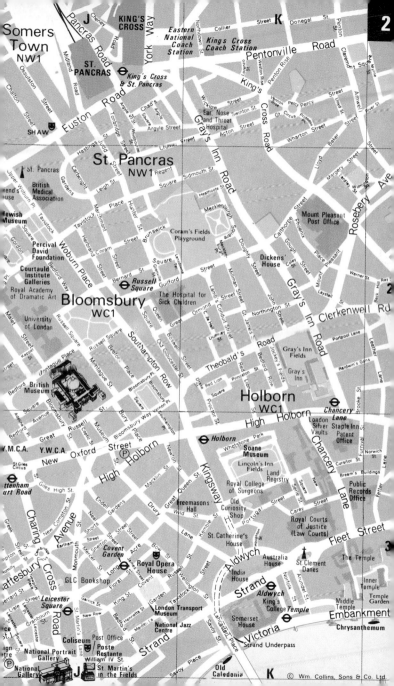

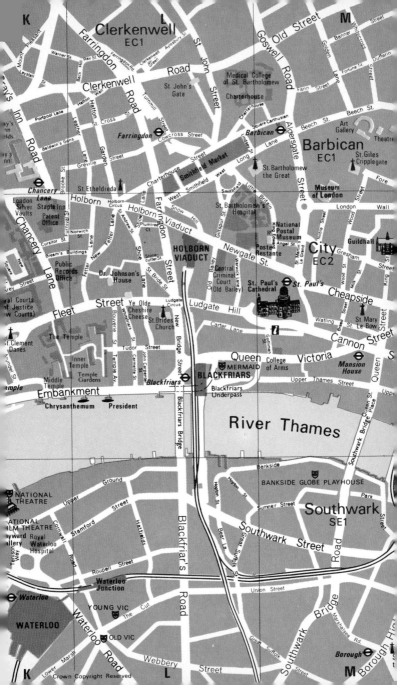

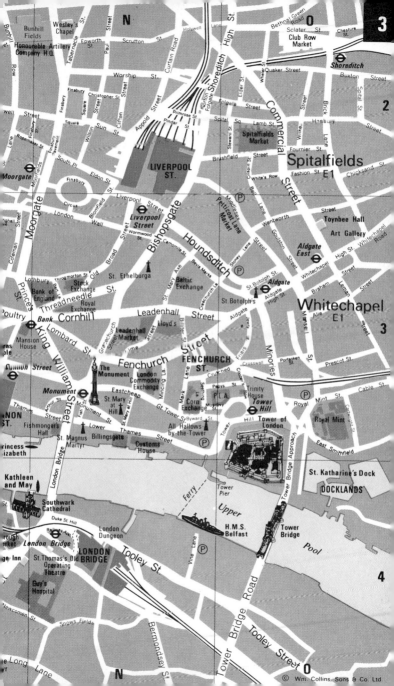

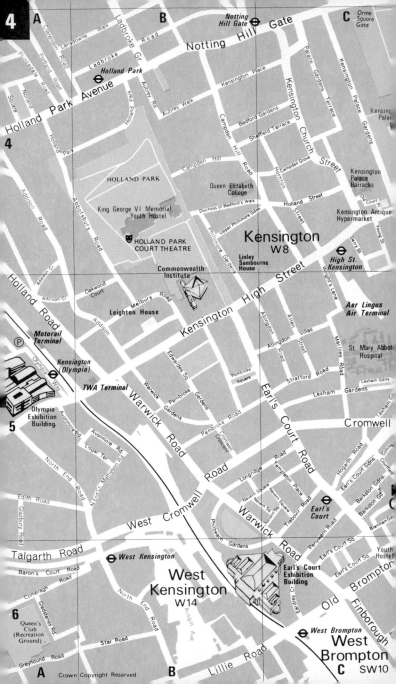

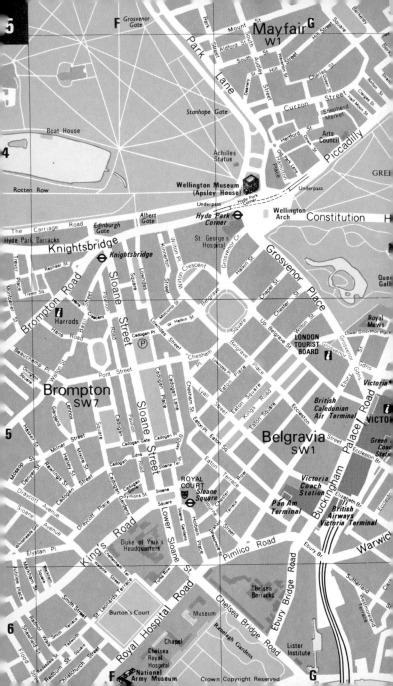

6

© Wm. Collins, Sons & Co. Ltd.

MUSEUMS AND GALLERIES

The majority of museums, galleries and places of interest charge for admission. Group rates are usually available on request. Most museums and galleries are closed on New Year's Day, Christmas Day, Boxing Day. On public holidays arrangements vary.

For the latest information and opening times a preliminary enquiry at the LVCB Tourist Information Centre is advisable. 730 3488, Mon.—Sat. 0900—2030.

The bus route numbers and Underground stations given with each entry are all within a maximum of five minutes' walk.

Alexandra Palace TV Museum Muswell Hill N10. New museum opening in 1988 on site of first BBC TV transmitter. British Rail Kings Cross to Alexandra Palace.

Artillery Museum Woolwich Common SE18. Guns, muskets, rifles and modern weapons on display, housed in a tent-like building originally erected in St James's Park in 1814 for the reception of the allied sovereigns of Europe in the final stages of the Napoleonic wars. Mon.—Fri. 1200—1600 or 1700; Sat. and Sun. 1300—1600. Bus 53. Underground New Cross, then bus.

Baden-Powell House Queen's Gate SW7. With a statue to the founder of the Boy Scouts in the foreground, this building, HQ of the movement, has an interesting array of mementos, trophies and historical records. Mon.—Sat. 0900—2000. Bus 49, 74. Underground Gloucester Rd.

Bankside Gallery 48 Hopton St. SE1. Changing exhibits of water colours and prints by two societies of artists. Tues.—Sat. 1000—1700 and Sun. 1400—1800. Bus 17, 44, 70. Underground Blackfriars or Mansion House.

HMS Belfast Symon's Wharf, Vine Lane, SE1. Moored on the south side of the Thames close to Tower Bridge HMS *Belfast*, the last of the Royal Navy's big-gun cruisers, is a floating museum housing memories of naval actions during the Second World War. The exhibits are regularly changed to reflect a particular facet of war at sea, and the ship can be explored from stem to stern. Daily. 1100—1630 (or sunset in winter). Bus 42, 47, 70, 78, 188. Underground London Bridge or Tower Hill.

Bethnal Green Museum of Childhood Cambridge Heath Rd E2. A delightful museum in a building first erected in Kensington as the original Victoria and Albert Museum. It is the best surviving example of the glass and iron construction used for the Great Exhibition of 1851. It has a fascinating collection of toys, games, dolls' houses, model theatres, books and children's clothes. Mon.—Thurs. and Sat. 1000—1800, Sun. 1430—1800. Bus 8, 106, 253. Underground Bethnal Green.

British Museum Great Russell St. WC1. Regarded as the greatest, and certainly the largest, museum in the world, the 'BM' was founded in 1753 to house the collections and libraries of distinguished donors, including George II, who presented books collected by generations of English monarchs. The main part of the present building was completed in 1847, with additions built in 1857, 1882, 1914 and 1938.

It is claimed that day-long visits for a week would be needed even to make a cursory examination of this palace of the world's treasures and history. For the visitor with only a few hours to spare there are conducted tours several times a day to view either the most notable exhibits or a particular category of interest. Those who prefer to go on their own will find it useful to know the classification of departments under Roman numerals I to XI. They are: **I** Printed books. **II** Manuscripts. **III** Oriental printed books and manuscripts. **IV** Prints and drawings. **V** Medals and coins. **VI** Egyptian antiquities. **VII** Western Asiatic antiquities. **VIII** Greek and Roman antiquities. **IX** British and medieval antiquities. **X** Oriental antiquities. **XI** Ethnography and research laboratories.

Departments **III** and **IV** are closed in 1988 to enable a new gallery to be built on the original roof to show the Japanese collection of ancient and contemporary art.

The visitor with a special interest can therefore make his way to the rooms of the department concerned. For those who wish to see the variety of outstanding exhibits, irrespective of kind or origin, here is a survey of the basic layout of the Museum.

Coming through the main entrance, to the left of the entrance hall are Greek and Roman antiquities, with figures and pottery from Minoa and Mycenae. Notable are the 5th-century BC sculptures of Apollo. The famous Elgin Marbles from the Parthenon at Athens are in a specially constructed gallery. Among the Roman exhibits — the largest collection in any of the world's museums — perhaps the most notable is the Portland Vase, made in two layers of glass more than 2000 years ago.

Adjacent to these rooms are the massive sculptures from Assyria, many of them from Nineveh, and next to them galleries devoted to Egyptian antiquities. Focus of interest amid the enormous sculptures of the Pharaohs and Egyptian gods is the Rosetta Stone which, with its inscription in three languages (two Egyptian and one Greek), provided the key to translating Egyptian hieroglyphics, when it was discovered in the waters of the Nile in 1798.

To the right, and behind the Reading Room (used only by ticket holders), are rooms exhibiting books and manuscripts. Among the treasures are the earliest known copies of the *Odyssey* and the *Iliad*; the illuminated Lindisfarne Gospels of the 8th century; an 11th-century manuscript of the *Saxon Chronicle*; the *Codex Sinaiticus*, a 4th-century Greek manuscript of the Bible; the manuscript of the Wycliffe Bible, the first written in English; and the article prepared by the Barons as the basis for Magna Carta.

Autographed documents include one signed by Shakespeare, the log book of Nelson describing naval tactics for the Battle of Trafalgar, and a host of papers with the signatures of the famous from history – Mary Queen of Scots, Cromwell and Wellington among them.

Among the Oriental exhibits is a Chinese scroll of 868, believed to be the earliest printed manuscript in existence.

Stairs lead to the upper floor. In the section over the main entrance are exhibits from prehistoric and Roman Britain. Of particular interest is the beautifully designed Roman silverware of the Mildenhall treasure, and the ornaments and weapons from the Sutton Hoo ship burial, the funerary gifts for an East Anglian chieftain.

Beyond this section is the collection of coins and medals covering all periods of history and all countries, exhibits of clocks and watches, and rooms devoted to objects from medieval Britain. The galleries in this part of the Museum are used for regularly changed displays of special interest, a 'museum within a museum', and many visitors regard this as the ideal part to visit if time is limited.

The rear of the upper floor displays antiquities from Anatolia, Babylon, and Upper Egypt. Rooms 60 and 61 have the mummies and mummy cases, and the exhibits include an ox believed to be the Golden Calf of the Old Testament. Babylonian exhibits include objects from Ur of the Chaldees.

You can take an elevator, or stairs, to the Edward VII extension opened in 1914. One floor is devoted to Asian civilization from prehistory to modern times. The pottery, jade and glassware of China are of particular interest, reflecting the country's artistic life from 5000 BC to the 20th century. Of equal appeal are the exquisite examples of Japanese art evident even in the manufacture of armour which was as beautiful as it was practical.

Next to the section of Oriental paintings, the collection of European prints and drawings displays a selection, regularly changed, from the Museum's enormous total of paintings, woodcuts, etchings and engravings representative of the finest work of British and European artists from the 15th century to the present day. **2** J2

Mon.-Sat. 1000–1700, Sun. 1430–1800. Bus 7, 8, 19, 22, 24, 25, 29, 38, 68, 73, 77, 170, 172, 176, 188. Underground Goodge St., Holborn, Russell Sq. or Tottenham Court Rd.

British Museum

Burlington House Piccadilly W1. Originally built in 1664 as the town residence of Richard Boyle, Earl of Burlington, a great patron of the arts, the present building is just over a century old and incorporates part of the original house. It is the home of a number of learned societies, including the Royal Academy of Arts. On the upper floors is a permanent exhibition of paintings, and every summer, from May to August, new work is shown. Any artist is entitled to submit pictures for viewing by a committee, though inevitably only a few are rewarded by having their work exhibited. For the rest of the year regular exhibitions of the world's greatest paintings are held. **5** H4

Mon.-Sat. 1000–1800, Sun. 1400–1800. Bus 9, 14, 19, 22, 25, 38. Underground Piccadilly Circus.

Carlyle's House 24 Cheyne Row SW3. The home of Thomas Carlyle and his wife Jane from 1834 until his death 47 years

later. Here is the desk at which he sat while writing his biography of Frederick the Great and his history of the French Revolution. Almost everything is preserved just as the Carlyles knew it.
Wed.-Sat. 1100–1700, Sun. 1400–1700 or sunset if earlier (Apr.-Oct.). Bus 11, 19, 22, 39, 45, 49. Underground Sloane Sq.

Commonwealth Institute 230 Kensington High St. W8. Housed in one of the most spectacular public buildings erected since the war, with finance and material supplied by the nations of the British Commonwealth, the Institute has three galleries under a vast copper-sheathed roof. The object of the exhibition is to illustrate the history and geography of the Commonwealth. There are also art exhibitions, a cinema and library. Displays are constantly changed and there are regular conducted tours, lectures and educational sessions **4** B4
Mon.-Sat. 1000–1630, Sun, 1400–1700. Bus 9, 27, 28, 31, 33, 49, 73. Underground Kensington High St.

Courtauld Institute Woburn Sq. WC1. Regarded as the most comprehensive collection of the works of Impressionist and post-Impressionist artists in Britain, including works by Manet, Renoir, Cézanne, Monet, Degas, Modigliani, Utrillo and van Gogh. Other rooms display works by old masters such as Veronese, Botticelli, Goya and Rubens, as well as period furniture. Bequests, intended to further the Institute's purpose in serving as an art gallery for London University, have added African sculptures, British art prior to 1914, and medieval paintings, glassware and enamels from Italy and France. Plans were announced in 1983 to move most of the collection to Somerset House (p. 56). **2** J2
Mon.-Sat. 1000–1700, Sun. 1400–1700. Bus 14, 24, 68, 73, 77, 170, 176, 188. Underground Euston Sq., Goodge St. or Russell Sq.

Cuming Museum Walworth Road SE17. This out-of-the-way museum reflects the devotion to London's history by one family from the 18th century onwards. It is essentially a museum for those intrigued by the history of London and Londoners; it contains Roman and medieval relics.
Mon.-Fri. 1000–1730, Sat. 1000–1700. Bus 12, 17, 35, 40, 45, 68, 171, 176, 184. Underground Elephant and Castle.

Design Centre 28 Haymarket SW1. A regular source of an interesting half hour or so, as the display is frequently changed to show the best and latest in British design and manufacture. Exhibits are almost entirely consumer goods, both mass-produced and craftsman-made.

Every product on show has attained a standard of quality approved by the semi-official Design Council. **2** J3
Mon.-Sat. 0930–1730 (to 2100 Wed. and Thurs.). Bus 3, 6, 9, 12, 13, 14, 15, 19, 22, 38, 53, 88, 159. Underground Piccadilly Circus.

Dickens' House 48 Doughty St. WC1. Charles Dickens lived here while he was writing *Oliver Twist*, *Nicholas Nickleby* and *Barnaby Rudge*. Although for many years the terraced house was in private hands, it was taken over in 1924 by the Dickens Fellowship and restored as accurately as possible to its appearance when Dickens and his increasing family lived there. There are many unique relics including letters, portraits and personal possessions. The basement kitchen is of interest as a replica of that of Dingley Dell in *Pickwick Papers*. **2** K2
Mon.-Sat. 1000–1700. Bus 17, 18, 19, 38, 45, 46, 55, 172. Underground Russell Sq.

Donaldson Museum Prince Consort Road SW7. This museum is in the Royal College of Music building. It contains a collection of old string and wind instruments, and early types of piano.
Mon. and Wed. 1030–1630 in term time after written application to Curator. Bus 9, 14, 30, 45, 49, 52, 73, 74. Underground South Kensington.

Dulwich Art Gallery College Road SE21. The first public picture gallery in the London area, opened in 1814, it was largely rebuilt after damage by a rocket in 1944. Valuable paintings of the Dutch, Italian, Spanish and French schools are on show, as well as many of the original 16th- and early 17th-century portraits used to illustrate Shakespeare's works and Elizabethan history books.
Tues.-Sat. 1000–1700, Sun. 1400–1700. Opening times vary in winter (tel. 693 5254). Bus 12, 78, 176, 185. Underground Brixton, then bus 3.

Film Archives 81 Dean St. W1. Large collection of cinema films and recorded TV programmes, along with posters and stills, organized by the British Film Institute. Prior enquiry necessary.
Mon.-Sat. 1000–1800. Bus 7, 8, 14, 19, 22, 23, 38. Underground Piccadilly Circus or Tottenham Court Rd.

Freud Museum 20 Maresfield Gardens, Hampstead NW3. In 1938, after the annexation of Austria by Nazi Germany, Sigmund Freud moved to London. The home of the pioneer psychoanalyst, containing his library and archaeological collection, was preserved by his daughter Anna after his death in 1939.
Mon.–Sat. 1000–1700, Sun. 1300–1700. Underground Finchley Rd. Bus 13, 28, 46.

Friends House Euston Rd NW1. HQ of the Society of Friends (Quakers). Among the unique collection of historic treasures is the journal kept by the founder, George Fox, first published in 1694.　**2 J2**
Inspection after prior written application. Bus 14, 18, 30, 68, 77, 170, 188. Underground Euston or Euston Sq.

Geffrye Museum Kingsland Rd E2. One of the least-known and most delightful museums off the beaten track in London. Originally built by a Lord Mayor of London, in 1715, as a rural retreat for the aged, it has been transformed with a minimum of modernization into a series of period rooms each meticulously furnished with the appropriate furniture and utensils.
Tues.–Sat. 1000–1700, Sun. 1400–1700. Bus 8, 106. Underground Liverpool Street, then bus 22, 48.

Geological Museum Exhibition Rd SW7. In a series of displays on the lower floor, the long story of the Earth is told, from probable origin to the present day. The rest of the exhibition is concerned with the terrain of the British Isles, its minerals, water, rock formations and alluvial deposits, and there is a superb collection of gemstones. In the main hall is a tiny piece of the moon brought back by the Apollo 16 astronauts. The reference library contains 70,000 books and 28,000 maps.　**4 D5**
Mon.–Sat. 1000–1800, Sun. 1430–1800. Bus 14, 30, 45, 49, 74. Underground South Kensington.

Goldsmith's Hall Foster Lane (off Gresham St.) EC2. Antique plate and the largest collection of modern silver and jewellery in Britain. Periodic special exhibitions (information on tel. 606 8971). Visits by appointment. Bus 6, 8, 9, 11, 15, 21, 22, 23, 43, 76, 133. Underground Bank, Mansion House or St Paul's.

Guildhall Gresham St. EC2. This 15th-century centre of London City's government, largely destroyed by fire in 1666 and severely damaged in 1940 air raids, remains the oldest and finest building in the City. Its Great Hall, scene of many trials for treason and religious offences in times gone by, includes memorials to many national figures such as Nelson, Wellington and Sir Winston Churchill. Ad-joining is an art gallery, where both old and new works of art concerned with the City are exhibited. A modern extension houses a library of 150,000 volumes and a collection of clocks and watches.　**3 M3**
Mon.–Sat. 1000–1700 and Sun. May–Sept. 1000–1700 (gallery closed between exhibitions). Bus 6, 8, 9, 11, 15, 21, 22, 23, 25, 43, 76, 133. Underground Bank or Mansion House.

Guinness World of Records Exhibition Trocadero Centre, Piccadilly Circus, W1. Life-size models, videos and computers bringing to life the amazing facts of the Guinness books, divided into six themes. Daily 1000–2130. Bus 13, 14, 15, 19, 22, 38. Underground Piccadilly Circus.

Hayward Gallery Belvedere Rd SE1. In a river setting, this gallery is part of the South Bank Arts Centre, and the principal 'shop window' for artistic work supported by the Arts Council. As well as picture galleries there are sculptures in the open air.　**6 K4**
Mon.–Wed. 1000–2000. Thurs.–Sat. 1000–1800, Sun. 1200–1800. Closed between exhibitions. Bus 1, 4, 68, 70, 76, 149, 168, 171, 176, 188. Underground Waterloo.

Heinz Gallery 21 Portman Sq. W1. The historic collection of drawings and plans of the Royal Institute of British Architects is kept here.
Mon.–Fri. 1100–1700 (closed while exhibitions are changed). Bus 1, 2, 13, 26, 30, 59, 74, 113, 159. Underground Bond St. or Marble Arch.

Hogarth's House Hogarth Lane W4. The artist's home and studio for the last 15 years of his life, by which time his reputation as founder of a new school of British painting had been established.
Mon.–Sat. 1100–1800, Sun. 1400–1800. In winter, Mon.–Sat. 1100–1600 (closed Tues.), Sun. 1400–1600. Bus 290. Underground Hammersmith.

Horniman Museum 100 London Rd SE23. This Museum is the practical result of an enthusiastic collector sharing his treasures with the public. Presented to London by F. J. Horniman some 80 years ago, it houses a wide variety of exhibits showing early man's tools, religious objects and magical symbols. There is also a collection of musical instruments.
Mon.–Sat. 1030–1800, Sun. 1400–1800. Bus 12, 63, 176. British Rail Forest Hill.

Imperial Collection Central Hall Westminster SW1. Replicas of the crown jewels of the world. Mon.–Sat. 1000–1800. Bus 3, 11, 12, 24, 29, 53. Underground Westminster.

Imperial War Museum Lambeth Rd SE1. Set in a pleasant little park, the building was actually the notorious Bedlam, a hospital for the insane. The exhibits — models, dioramas and actual equipment — are concerned with all facets of war since 1914. The picture gallery has a splendid display of the best of official war artists, and the library of photographs and documents is the main source of information for historians. **6 L5** Mon.–Sat. 1000–1750, Sun. 1400–1750. Bus 1, 3, 10, 12, 17, 44, 45, 53, 59, 63, 109, 141, 155, 171, 172, 176, 184, 188. Underground Elephant and Castle.

Institute of Contemporary Arts Nash House, the Mall SW1. Displays regularly changed. Theatre and video library. Daily 1200–2300. Bus, 9, 14, 19, 22, 25. Underground Green Park.

Jewish Museum Woburn House, Tavistock Sq. WC1. Just one room houses many valuable relics of the religious history of the Jewish people. **2 J2** Tues.–Thurs. (Fri. in summer) 1000–1600, Sun. 1000–1245. Bus 14, 18, 30, 73, 77. Underground Euston Sq.

Dr Johnson's House Gough Square EC4. Remarkably, the air raids which devastated most of the warren of courts and alleys behind Fleet Street did only minor damage to Dr Samuel Johnson's house, and, just as fortunately, post-war development has not marred its 18th-century peace. **3 L3** Mon.–Sat. 1100–1730 (in winter 1700). Bus 4, 6, 9, 11, 15. Underground Blackfriars.

Keats' House Keats Grove, Hampstead NW3. The house, called Lawn Bank, was the home of the poet for two years, and it was here that he wrote *Ode to a Nightingale*. The house contains many documents, letters, and the script of his last work, *Bright Star*, on a blank page of his beloved copy of Shakespeare's works. Mon.–Sat. 1000–1300 and 1400–1800 Sun. 1400–1700. Bus 24, 46, 216, 237. Underground Hampstead.

Kensington Palace Kensington Gardens W8. Standing in an area of luxurious residences, including the embassies of the Soviet Union and France, the palace is mainly the work of Christopher Wren (exterior) and William Kent (interior). The Orangery was built in 1704, by Hawksmoor. Queen Victoria was born here, and mementos of her early life include her collection of dolls, contrasting with the unique ivory throne she was given as Queen Empress. Part of the palace is the residence of the Prince and Princess of Wales. **4 C4** Mon.–Sat. 0900–1700, Sun. 1300–1700 (last tickets 1615). Bus 9, 12, 27, 31, 49, 52, 73, 88. Underground Kensington High St. or Lancaster Gate.

Kenwood House and Gallery Hampstead Lane NW3. This 18th-century, Robert Adam mansion, in the north-east corner of the Heath, is furnished as it was originally, and there are paintings by many old masters, including Vermeer, Gainsborough and Rembrandt. Daily 1000–1900 (Apr.–Sept.); 1000–1700 (Oct and Feb.–Mar); 1000–1600 (Nov.–Jan.). Bus 210. Underground Golders Green, then bus 210.

Kew Bridge Engines Museum Models and historic engines, including largest steam beam engine in the world. Daily 1100–1700 (engines in steam Sat. and Sun). British Rail Kew Bridge or Underground Gunnersbury (near), then bus 237, 267.

Lawn Tennis Museum Church Rd SW19. Right in the centre of the grounds of the All-England club, Wimbledon, this museum is the only one of its kind in the world. Tues.–Sat. 1100–1700, Sun. 1400–1700. Bus (near) 22, 28. Underground Southfields or Wimbledon.

Light Fantastic: World Centre of Holography 13 Coventry St. W1. Use of holograms in science and industry. Daily 1000–2200 Bus 3, 6, 9, 12, 13, 14, 15, 88. Underground Piccadilly Circus.

London Diamond Centre 10 Hanover St. W1. Exhibition of methods of diamond mining, cutting, polishing etc. and displays of diamond jewellery. Mon.–Fri. 0930–1730, Sat. 0930–1330. Bus 6, 7, 8, 13, 15. Underground Oxford Circus.

London Dungeon 28 Tooley St. SE1. Tableaux of mediaeval prison (unsuitable for young children). April–Sept. Daily 1000–1730, Oct.–Mar. 1000–1630. Bus 42, 47, 70, 133. Underground London Bridge.

London, Museum of London Wall EC2 A newly built museum, this is the best place to appreciate the long and spectacu-

Museum of London

lar history of London over some 2000 years from the Stone, Bronze and Iron Ages, a 1st-century Roman ewer engraved *Londini* (first known reference to the City's name), to the first Ford car made in England and the Lord Mayor's coach. The treasures excavated on the site of the Temple of Mithras in Queen Victoria St., interiors of workshops, shops and houses

spanning the centuries, and a display of costumes are among the other exhibits.
3 M2
Tues.—Sat. 1000—1800, Sun. 1400—1800. Bus 4, 141, 502. Underground Barbican, Moorgate or St Paul's.

London Silver Vaults   53 Chancery Lane WC2. For more than 90 years these strongrooms have been the storehouse for silverware, most of it antique, with some fine examples of modern work.   **2 K3** Mon.-Fri. 0900–1730, Sat. 0900–1230. Bus 8, 22, 25. Underground Chancery Lane.

London Toy and Model Museum 23 Craven Hill W2. Two major toy collections; one of pre-1914 toys and the other of working model trains.
Tues.—Sat. 1000—1730, Sun. 1100—1730. Bus 12, 27, 88. Underground Lancaster Gate or Queensway.

London Transport Museum This collection of historic horse-drawn passenger vehicles, buses, trams and underground trains, with scale models of rolling stock, vehicles, stations, *etc*, and displays of old posters is established in the old flower market in Covent Garden.   **2 J3** Daily 1000–1800. Bus 1, 6, 9, 11, 13, 15, 24, 29, 77. Underground Covent Garden.

Marlborough House Pall Mall SW1. Designed by Christopher Wren for the Duke of Marlborough, it was the London home of Edward VII and George V before their accession.   **5 H4** Visits Mon.—Fri. by prior application (tel. 930 9249). Bus 9, 14, 19, 22, 25, 38. Underground Green Pk.

Museum of Design Butler's Wharf SE1. New museum (1988) devoted to modern industrial design. Enquire at LVCB offices for opening hours. Bus 42, 47, 78. Underground London Bridge.

Museum of Garden History St Mary's, Lambeth Palace Rd SE1. Rare plants and 17th century botanical garden. Apr.—Nov. Mon.—Fri. 1100—1500, Sun. 1030—1700. Bus 3, 10, 44, 76. Underground Lambeth North.

Museum of Mankind   6 Burlington Gardens W1. This spectacular branch of the British Museum shows, in a style as modern as most of the exhibits are old, the ethnic story of man. It is regarded as the most comprehensive collection in existence of the tribal and folk arts and crafts of all the world's peoples. There are free film shows to delight and educate both young and old.   **2 H3** Mon.-Sat. 1000–1700, Sun. 1430–1800. Bus 9, 14, 19, 22, 25, 38. Underground Piccadilly Circus or Green Pk.

Museum of Moving Image South Bank SE1 (next to National Film Theatre). Displays of film, TV and video apparatus.

Enquire at LVCB offices for tickets. Bus 1, 4, 68, 70. Underground Waterloo.

Musical Museum   368 High St., Brentford. Fine working organs, pianolas and other mechanical musical instruments. Sat.-Sun. 1400–1700 (Apr.-Oct.). Underground South Ealing, then bus 65.

National Gallery Trafalgar Sq. WC2. First opened in 1838, it has been periodically enlarged to house its enormous collection of the world's masterpieces of painting, the most recent extension being completed in 1976. Even so, it is only possible for about 2000 of its 4500 pictures to be displayed in the public rooms, though these exhibits are changed.

Before entering the building visitors will note two statues standing on the manicured lawns on either side of the entrance. One is of James II wearing Roman costume, the other is a copy of the George Washington statue which stands in Richmond, Virginia.

No one, unless proposing to spend several days in the Gallery, should attempt to look at all the pictures — one of the most valuable and finest collections of art in the world. It is best to join one of the lecture tours held on most days, starting at 1300, usually concentrating on one artist or school of art, or to decide on a particular interest and devote one's visit solely to that. All the rooms are numbered according to the school exhibited in them. The list below indicates the numbering system. By turning left from the entrance hall, the sequence is roughly in a clockwise direction, with 1—15 leading to 16—27.

In the main building 28–46 brings you back to the entrance hall.

The following details indicate the schools in the rooms. Only a small proportion of the artists whose works are displayed can be mentioned in a brief survey.

Rooms 1–15, 29–31, 35, 37–39 Works by Fra Angelico, Giotto, Botticelli, da Vinci, Michelangelo, Bellini, Giorgione, Correggio, Raphael, Caravaggio, Canaletto, and numerous other masters of the Italian schools of Siena, Florence, Venice, Lombardy, Verona, *etc*. These rooms display some of the Gallery's most famous pictures, notably Fra Angelico's *Christ in Glory*, da Vinci's *Virgin and Child with St John the Baptist and St Anne*, and *The Adoration of the Magi* by Veronese.

Rooms 16–19 and 25–28 No one should miss these rooms, with priceless masterpieces of the Dutch school: Franz Hals, Vermeer, and a collection of works by Rembrandt, including *Belshazzar's Feast*, two self-portraits, *Saskia as Flora*, and *The Woman Taken in Ad:ltery*.

Rooms 20–22 Works from the Flemish school, notably Rubens and van Dyck.

Room 23 has works by Dutch painters of the 15th and 16th centuries – Hieronymus Bosch, Pieter Brueghel, van Eyck and van der Weyden.

Room 24 displays paintings by Dürer and Holbein the Younger, among other artists of the early German school

Rooms 32, 33, 36, 40, 44–46 contain the finest of the Gallery's acquisitions representing the French school. Artists include Lorraine, Millet, Fragonard, Watteau, Corot, Delacroix, Ingres, Cézanne, Gauguin, Manet, Monet, Renoir, Rousseau, Sisley, van Gogh, and Toulouse-Lautrec. Some of the Impressionist and post-Impressionist works are periodically exchanged with the National Gallery in Dublin under the terms of the bequest of the original owner.

Room 34 is devoted to British artists. Constable's best-known landscapes are here, as well as portraits by Gainsborough, Hogarth's paintings of *Marriage à la Mode* (the six pictures which formed the nucleus of the Gallery's exhibits back in 1824), portraits by Reynolds, Stubbs' paintings of the horse, and typical works by Turner.

Rooms 41–43 show pictures from the Spanish school, including Goya's *Duke of Wellington*, stolen in 1961 and then returned. Other artists represented are El Greco, Murillo, and Velazquez whose picture, *The Rokeby Venus*, is of interest aside from its superb artistry; it was restored after damage by a suffragette campaigning for women's emancipation in 1914. **5** J4

Weekdays 1000–1800, Sun. 1400–1800. Bus 1, 3, 6, 9, 11, 12, 13, 15, 24, 29, 39, 53, 59, 77, 88, 159, 168, 170, 176. Underground Charing Cross.

National Maritime Museum Romney Rd, Greenwich SE10. Well worth a day-long visit, especially if combined with a

National Gallery

return river trip from Westminster Pier. Standing behind the Royal Naval College, the museum occupies two buildings. One is built around the Queen's House (designed by Inigo Jones in 1617), the other is in the old Royal Observatory. There are actual vessels and ships' models from prehistory to today; maps, atlases, charts, navigational instruments and chronometers, uniforms (including Nelson's at Trafalgar); a superb collection of portraits and seascapes by such masters as Lely, Reynolds, Romney and Gainsborough – everything to tell the story of British maritime power.

Behind Flamsteed House, part of the old Royal Observatory (now removed to clearer atmosphere at Herstmonceux in Sussex), is the brass strip which marks the Greenwich Meridian and the division of the world into east and west hemispheres.

Alongside the river pier a tour of inspection may be made of *Gipsy Moth IV*, Sir Francis Chichester's round-the-world yacht, and *Cutty Sark*, preserved as the finest example of the tea clippers which plied between China and England more than a century ago.

Museum and Observatory Mon.–Sat. 1000–1800, Sun. 1400–1700. *Gipsy Moth IV* Mon.–Thurs. 1100–1700, Sat. 1430–1700 (not Sun.); and *Cutty Sark* weekdays 1100–1700, Sun. 1430–1700. Bus 53, 54, 75, 177, 180, 185. Underground Surrey Docks, then bus. River boats Westminster and Tower Piers.

National Portrait Gallery St Martin's Place WC2. Tucked away behind the National Gallery, the accent here is on historical appeal rather than artistic quality – though it should be stressed that many of the pictures are by great artists, including Holbein, van Dyck, Romney and Gainsborough.

Apart from the royal family, there are no portraits of anyone living, but there are many famous faces from the past. Fame is not the only criterion, notoriety may also merit the inclusion of a portrait. Thus, while Charles II is on view, so are his mistresses, including Nell Gwyn. The Gallery offers a unique opportunity to look at the faces of men and women from history – Shakespeare, Pepys, Cromwell, Handel, Wordsworth, the Brontë sisters (painted by their brother Bramwell), and almost every leading statesman, churchman, inventor, scientist, artist and musician of the past three centuries. Though the majority of portraits are of personalities from British history, exceptions are the inclusion of portraits of Benjamin Franklin and George Washington.

Generally the portraits are hung in chronological order, starting with the heads on coins of the Anglo-Saxon kings (the only portraits in existence). The earliest original picture is of Henry III, painted in the 13th century, and Henry VII is the subject of the earliest painting from life, when the king was 48, in 1505.

Among the other royal portraits are those of Henry VIII and three of his wives, Mary Queen of Scots, Elizabeth I, Charles I and his queen, Queen Victoria and Prince Albert, George V and Queen Mary, Annigoni's portrait of Elizabeth II and Organ's portraits of the Prince and Princess of Wales. **2 J3**
Mon.–Fri. 1000–1700, Sat. 1000–1800, Sun. 1400–1800. Bus 1, 3, 6, 9, 11, 12, 13, 15, 24, 29, 39, 53, 59, 159, 168, 170, 176. Underground Leicester Sq.

Natural History Museum Cromwell Rd SW7. This superb collection, actually part of the British Museum, is housed in an impressive building characteristic of late Victorian style. There are five sections – zoology, entomology, palaeontology, mineralogy, and botany. As one of the world's most important research centres in these subjects, the museum offers unique opportunities for the serious student and expert, but its spectacular exhibits, such as a quarter of a million different butterflies, fossilized skeletons of prehistoric monsters, and the full-scale cast of a whale, plus plants and blossoms from all over the world, offer plenty of interest for everyone. There is a section specially for children, where they can obtain sketching pads and pencils to make a personal memento of their visit. **4 D5**
Mon.–Sat. 1000–1800, Sun. 1430–1800. Bus 14, 30, 45, 49, 74. Underground South Kensington.

Operating Theatre Old St Thomas's Hospital, the Chapter House, St Thomas St. SE1. Restored women's operating theatre of 1822, then the only specially built operating theatre in England. Exhibits show the history of surgery and herbal medicine over the centuries. Usually open Mon., Wed. and Fri. 1230–1600; Tues. and Thurs. after 1130 by appointment only for groups. Preliminary enquiry advisable. 407 7600 Ext. 2739. Bus 10, 17, 21, 40, 42. Underground London Bridge.

Order of St John Museum St John's Lane EC1. Housed in the 16th-century gatehouse of a 12th-century priory destroyed by fire in 1381, the museum records the history of the Knights Hospitallers, with silver, paintings and other treasures. The adjoining church is open to visitors. Museum open Tues. and Fri. 1000–1800, Sat. 1000–1600. Explanatory tours lasting 1 hour Tues., Fri. and Sat. 1100 and 1430. Underground Farringdon. Bus 5, 55, 63, 221, 243.

Percival David Foundation 53 Gordon Sq. WC1. A small museum housing one of the best collections of Chinese ceramics in the West. The exhibits span more than a thousand years of manufacture, and most of the pieces were originally owned by Chinese emperors. The Foundation also contains a large reference library. **2 J2**
Mon. 1400–1700, Tues.–Fri. 1030–1700, Sat. 1030–1300. Bus 14, 24, 29, 68, 73, 77, 170, 176, 188. Underground Euston Sq.

Planetarium Marylebone Rd NW1. Beneath a huge dome a projector shows celestial bodies to an accurate scale as regards movement, size, distance and brightness. Displays are hourly, accompanied by a commentary. **1 F2**
Daily 1100–1630. Bus 1, 2, 13, 18, 26, 27, 30, 59, 74, 113, 176.

Pollock's Toy Museum 1 Scala St. W1. Games, dolls, dolls' houses, mechanical toys, and toy theatres are some of the examples of the things which delighted children up to a century ago. There is also a shop selling dolls' house furniture, jigsaws, and model theatres. **2 H2**
Mon.-Sat. 1000–1700. Bus 14, 24, 29, 73, 176. Underground Goodge St.

Postal Museum King Edward St. EC1. Housed in the building of the London Chief Post Office, where the world's first prepaid postal service began, this museum is a must for every stamp collector. There are exhibits of about 400,000 stamps with a value beyond assessment. Though organized by the Post Office, the collection is not restricted to British stamps, but includes examples from all over the world. **3 M3**
Mon.–Thurs. 1000–1630 (Fri. 0930–1600). Bus 4, 8, 22, 25, 141. Underground St Paul's.

Public Records Office Chancery Lane WC2. Part of this building, in which national records since the Norman Conquest are stored, has been arranged as a museum. Exhibits include the Domesday Book, completed in 1086, with a modern copy which can be examined. Here one can see Guy Fawkes' signature on the Gunpowder Plot plans, the Papal bull making Henry VIII defender of the faith, the signatures of the kings and queens of England, Shakespeare and William Penn, the *Victory*'s log kept during the Battle of Trafalgar and more recent documents. **3 K3**
Mon.–Fri. 1300–1600. Bus 4, 6, 9, 11, 15, 171, Underground Chancery Lane.

Queen's Gallery Buckingham Palace Rd SW1. The annex on the east side of the Palace was once the monarch's private chapel. In 1962, in order to allow the public to see some of the superb paintings in the Royal Collection, the Queen had the

building adapted as a gallery in which artistic treasures, brought from all the royal palaces, could be seen by the public. Pictures are regularly changed.   **5 G4**
Tues.-Sat. 1100–1700, Sun. 1400–1700. Bus 2, 11, 14, 16, 19, 22, 24, 25, 26, 29, 30, 36, 38, 39, 52. Underground St James's Park or Victoria

RAF Museum Hendon NW9. One of the newest and most popular of London's museums, opened on the site of the airfield which saw the birth of the Royal Air Force in 1918. There are three separate exhibitions: RAF history, Battle of Britain and Bomber Command. Some 50 aircraft of the past 65 years on show, including Hurricane, Spitfire, Wellington and Lancaster. Mon.–Sat. 1000–1800, Sun. 1400–1800. Underground Colindale.

Royal College of Surgeons' Museum Lincoln's Inn Fields WC2. A small museum in honour of John Hunter, the 18th-century founder of surgical pathology. In his lifetime he collected more than 13,000 specimens which were bequeathed to the College. Sadly, many of the exhibits were destroyed during an air raid in 1941.   **2 K3**
Open to members of the medical profession and to others by prior application (tel. 405 3474). Bus 8, 22, 25, 55, 68, 77, 170, 172, 188. Underground Holborn or Chancery Lane

Royal Geographical Society Library Kensington Gore SW7. This is really a museum of maps - more than half a million of them - with mementos of expeditions and explorations supported by the society since it started in 1830.
      4 D4
Mon.-Fri. 0930–1730. Bus 9, 53, 73. Underground South Kensington.

Royal Hospital Museum Chelsea Embankment SW3. This home of the famous red-coated Chelsea Pensioners, aged or invalid ex-soldiers, was reputedly built by Charles II at the request of his mistress Nell Gwyn. Though damaged during air raids, it has been carefully restored to its elegance as envisaged by Christopher Wren. Visitors may enter the beautiful chapel and Pensioners' dining room, noting the portraits of the succession of monarchs who have been the hospital's patrons, before entering the small museum, which tells the story of the Pensioners and their home.   **5 F6**
Adjacent, in a building as modern as the Hospital is old, is the **National Army Museum**, opened in 1971, showing exhibits connected with the army from 1485 – the year of the Battle of Bosworth and the beginning of the Tudor monarchy – to the outbreak of the First World War. A new wing was added in 1981.   **5 F6**

Royal Hospital: Weekdays 1000–1200 and 1400–1600, Sun. 1400–1600 in summer. National Army Museum: Mon.–Sat. 1000–1730, Sun. 1400–1730. Bus 11, 39, 137. Underground Sloane Sq.

Royal Mews Buckingham Palace Rd SW1. The mews is, of course, part of Buckingham Palace. Here you can see the Gold State Coach built to the order of George III and completed in 1761. It has been described as 'the most superb carriage ever built'. The Irish Coach, used for the State Opening of Parliament, horse-drawn carriages, and a number of the Queen's cars are also on view. An intriguing exhibit is Victoria's State Sleigh. The magnificent array of harness and saddlery is regarded as the best in the world.   **5 G5**
Wed. and Thurs. 1400–1600 (closed in Ascot Week). Bus 2, 11, 14, 16, 19, 22, 24, 25, 26, 29, 30, 36, 38, 39, 52. Underground St. James's Park or Victoria.

Science Museum Exhibition Road SW7. The term 'science' embraces every kind of invention and industrial enterprise, and the exhibits reflect both the triumphs of the past and the technological developments of today. Innumerable 'firsts' are on show – from quaint locomotives like *Puffing Billy* to Baird's first TV receiver, Whittle's jet engine, and the latest electronic marvels. Hundreds of models spring into activity at the touch of a button. There is also an impressive array of the inventions which have made the ordinary home the comfortable place it now is. A gallery designed for children has large dioramas portraying the development of energy sources and transport from prehistory till today.   **4 E5**
Mon.-Sat. 1000–1800, Sun. 1430–1800. Bus 14, 30, 45, 49, 74. Underground South Kensington.

Serpentine Gallery Kensington Gardens W2. Exhibitions, changed monthly, of contemporary British artists. building is a converted teahouse.   **4 E4**
Daily 1000–1900 (Apr.-Aug.); 1000–dusk (Sept.-Mar.). Bus 9, 52, 73. Underground Lancaster Gate.

Shakespeare Globe Museum Bear Gardens, Bankside SE1 is on the site of the original theatre. Replica of 16th-century playhouse. Opening times vary (enquiries 928 6342). Bus 17, 44, 70, 76. Underground London Bridge.

Soane Museum 13 Lincoln's Inn Fields WC2. Sir John Soane, one of the greatest architects at the turn of the 18th century, built this elegant house and filled it with antiques and pictures purchased during his lucrative career. The best known of his pictures are Hogarth's *Rake's Progress* and *The Election*, and notable works by Rey-

nolds and Turner. For the rest, the varied souvenirs of a wealthy traveller in Europe in Soane's day include Egyptian, Greek and Roman sculptures, while for the student of architecture there is the opportunity to see some of the 20,000 drawings Soane prepared. **2 K3**
Tues.-Sat. 1000–1700. Bus 8, 22, 25, 55, 68, 77, 170, 172, 188. Underground Holborn or Chancery Lane.

Somerset House Strand WC2. This huge building, on the site of the palace of the Duke of Somerset, Lord Protector of England during the brief reign of the boy king Edward VI, was begun in 1777, with two wings added in the 19th century. As it is the rear of the building which you see from the Strand, the superb front is best viewed from south of the river. The Inland Revenue is housed here. The wills of the famous once stored here have been transferred to the Public Records Office (p. 54), and the registers of births, marriages and deaths to 10 Kingsway. As a result of these removals the largest and most impressive rooms have been restored and are now used for exhibitions of paintings. The north block is due to house works of art hitherto displayed at the Courtauld Institute (p. 49). **2 K3**
Mon.-Fri. 1000–1630. Bus 1, 4, 6, 9, 11, 13, 15, 55, 68, 77, 170, 171, 172, 176, 188. Underground Temple.

South London Art Gallery Peckham Rd SE5. Originating as a cultural contribution in a shop owned by an art enthusiast, William Rossiter, over a century ago, this gallery has works by most of the best British artists of the period, including Millais, Leighton, G. F. Watts, and Ruskin. Modern works are added continually, and include those of Sickert and Piper.
Mon.-Sat. 1000–1800, Sun. 1500–1800 (periodically closed when exhibitions change). Bus 12, 36, 171. Underground Oval, then 36 bus; or Elephant and Castle, then 12 bus.

Stock Exchange Old Broad St. EC2. The nerve centre of the nation's dealings in stocks and shares is in a brand new building. The use of computers and Telex machines has abolished most of the previously hectic activity on the floor of the Exchange. **3 N3**
Mon.—Fri.0945—1515. Bus 6, 8, 9, 11, 15, 21, 22, 23, 25, 43, 76. Underground Bank.

Tate Gallery Millbank SW1. Four galleries in one building. The gallery of British art shows works from the past five centuries with notable masterpieces by Blake, Reynolds and Constable. The sculpture gallery includes works by Rodin, Epstein and Henry Moore. The modern foreign paintings section has many of the finest works of the Impressionists and post-Impressionists. Special exhibitions are constantly arranged, with loans from galleries all over the world, and many of these shows generate as much controversy as enthusiasm. The Tate has a busy and well-run restaurant. Even if a meal is not taken there it should be visited for the murals by Rex Whistler. The Clore gallery, opened in 1987, shows 200 of Turner's paintings and thousands of his drawings.
Mon.—Sat. 1000—1750, Sun. 1400—1750. Bus 76, 88, 159. Underground Pimlico.

Theatre Museum Russell St. WC2. Three galleries for historic and contemporary exhibits, small theatre, café and theatre ticket sales.

Louis XVI and family, Tussaud's

Tues.—Sat. 1100—1900 (Sun. shop, café and ticket sales only). Bus 1, 14, 19, 22, 24, 29, 38. Underground Covent Garden.

Tussaud's Marylebone Rd NW1. Although a commercial enterprise, Madame Tussaud's has become a national institution since the art mistress to Louis XVI of France fled to London during the Revolution, bringing with her the death masks of guillotined aristocrats she had been compelled to make. The macabre has remained a big attraction, with effigies — and authentic relics — of notorious criminals, but the more general appeal is in the meticulously executed wax replicas of famous people past and present. **1 F2**
Daily 1000–1830. Bus 1, 2, 13, 18, 26, 27, 30, 59, 74, 113, 159, 176. Underground Baker St.

Victoria and Albert Museum Cromwell Rd SW7. It would be frustrating to allow fewer than two half-day visits to this magnificent collection of all the decorative arts and crafts. Originating from the exhibits shown at the Great Exhibition of 1851, the museum opened in the present building in 1909, and is now regarded as the finest and largest collection of furnishings, textiles, costumes, carpets, jewellery, tapestry and glass in the world; there is also a fascinating theatre museum. Although the items span art over the centuries, generous tribute is made to all that is best in contemporary work from typography to fashion. For the serious student there are collections arranged according to subject, and what is regarded as the most comprehensive arts and crafts library in the world. **4 E5** Mon.-Thurs. and Sat. 1000–1750, Sun. 1430–1750. Bus 14, 30, 45, 49, 74. Underground South Kensington.

Wallace Collection Manchester Sq. W1. Just behind Selfridges in Oxford St. is the most valuable collection of treasures bequeathed to the nation by one person – the French wife of Sir Richard Wallace. The house itself is a fine example of an 18th-century town mansion, built for the Duke of Manchester. The exhibits which, under the terms of the bequest, can never be loaned, removed or augmented, are mostly of French 18th-century painting, sculpture, furniture, and porcelain. But there are also masterpieces from the English and Dutch schools (Franz Hals' *Laughing Cavalier* among them), medieval arms and armour, and *objets d'art* in gold. **2 G3** Mon.-Sat. 1000–1700. Sun. 1400–1700. Bus 1, 2, 6, 7, 8, 12, 13, 15, 26, 30, 59, 73, 74, 88, 137, Underground Bond St. or Marble Arch.

Wellcome Museum of the History of Medicine Exhibition Rd SW7. Transferred from its original site in the Wellcome Foundation's building, this museum is now within the Science Museum complex. Models and pictures illustrate the history of all branches of medicine through the ages, and there are replicas of chemists' shops and hospital wards, among the latter Joseph Lister's ward in a Glasgow hospital where he pioneered antiseptic surgery. Modern techniques include displays of heart transplant operations. A general section covers the art and science of healing. **4 E5** Mon.-Sat. 1000–1800, Sun. 1430–1800. Transport as for Science Museum.

Wellington Museum Hyde Park Corner W1. This late 18th-century mansion was bought by the Duke of Wellington after his victory at Waterloo ended the long war with Napoleon. The national hero's new home was promptly dubbed 'No. 1, London' by the public, and – semi-officially – it has remained so ever since. Most of the exhibits are trophies of the Iron Duke's career – uniforms, arms, medals, as well as pictures by Velazquez, Goya and Rubens. The hundreds of gifts showered on Wellington by the monarchs of liberated Europe are displayed. **5 F4** Tues., Thurs. and Sat. 1000–1800, Sun. 1430–1800. Bus 2, 9, 14, 16, 19, 22, 25, 26, 30, 36, 38, 52, 73, 74, 137. Underground Hyde Pk Corner.

Wesley's House and Chapel 47 City Rd EC1. This became the home of the founder of Methodism soon after his return from missionary work in America, and it holds a large collection of his personal possessions and relics of the early years of the movement. **3 N2** Mon.-Sat. 1000–1600 (other times by arrangement). Bus 5, 43, 55, 76, 104, 141. Underground Old St.

Whitechapel Art Gallery 80 Whitechapel High St. E1. Though off the usual tourist track, this is well worth discovering as it usually has one of the most interesting, if controversial, exhibitions of modern art in London. **3 O3** Sun.-Fri. 1100–1800 (closed between exhibitions). Tel. 377 0107. Bus 5, 10, 15, 23, 25, 40, 67. Underground Aldgate East.

William Morris Gallery Lloyd Park E17. A small building in honour of William Morris, Victorian advocate of combining art and industry, who was born in the district. Many of his designs for furniture, textiles, printing and wallpaper are on show, with pictures by Morris' friend, Brangwyn, the Belgian-born artist.

Mon., Wed., Fri., Sat. 1000–1700, Tues., Thurs. 1000–2000, first Sun. in month 1000–1200 and 1400–1700. Underground Walthamstow Central.

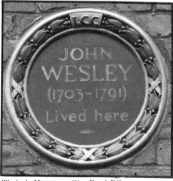

Wesley's House, 47 City Road EC1

The code references given in main entries refer to Central London maps between pages 36 and 46.

SHOPPING TOURS

The most comprehensive array of shops with popular appeal for both sexes, all ages and purses is in Oxford St. between Marble Arch and Oxford Circus. Here stand the large department and chain stores. Oxford St. also includes many shoe shops selling the best of British and continental footwear. Regent St. runs south from Oxford Circus. The shops here cater for many needs – from cosmetics and toys to furnishings and cars.

Turn right into Piccadilly where the shops are few but of a certain prestige, and include those selling books and high-quality foods. The shopper can then turn right into Bond St., where the accent is on luxury goods: ceramics, pictures, beauty accessories among them. At the top you are back in Oxford St. The total distance is only about 3km/2mi, but the attractions may make progress slow if rewarding.

The other major shopping districts are more concentrated. Brompton Rd is best known for Harrods, the palatial department store, and the Scotch House selling Scottish clothes and textiles. Kensington High St., with a number of large department stores and many boutiques, is less congested and compares with Oxford St. in popular appeal at keen prices. You can also pay a visit to the boutiques of the King's Rd, Chelsea by taking the 31 bus at the end of the shopping zone in Kensington High St.

A leisurely walk along King's Rd takes you to Sloane Square, with an attractive department store and many small shops offering everything from antiques to high – and exclusive – fashion. Continuing along Sloane St., Knightsbridge and Hyde Park Corner brings you full circle up Park Lane to Marble Arch.

Carriage trade in the West End

TOURS ON FOOT

Walks, with LVCB guides, lasting 1½–2 hours, are available daily. No booking needed. Meet at designated Underground station exit. Programmes from information offices.

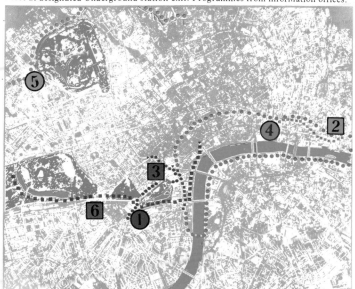

Royal London Tour

The royal aspect of London is contained within a short stroll which takes in the Changing of the Guard at Horse Guards or Buckingham Palace; Banqueting House, Marlborough House, Clarence House, St James's Palace, and the Queen's horses in the Royal Mews.

City Tour

Absorb the City's blend of history, religion and high finance in St Paul's Cathedral, St Vedast's church, St Mary Le Bow, the Guildhall, Bank of England, the Mansion House, official home of the Lord Mayor, the Monument and the Tower.

Floodlight Tour

The brightest lights in London are seen in the dazzle of neon signs in Piccadilly Circus. Public buildings, floodlit from dusk, include the National Gallery, Nelson's Column and the fountains in Trafalgar Square, Admiralty Arch, Houses of Parliament and Westminster Abbey.

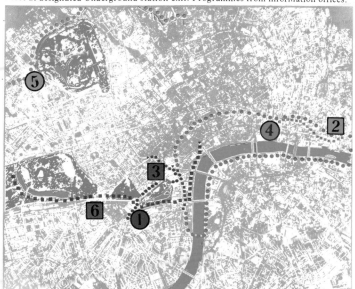 Silver Jubilee Walkway

This circular tour, charted in 1977–8 to celebrate the Queen's silver jubilee, shows examples of modern as well as historic London, and passes along both banks of the Thames. The route stretches for 15km 9mi but can be tackled in easy stages to suit a leisurely pace.

Towpath Walk

The towpath along Regent's Canal offers a tranquil stroll, 4km 2½mi, across the north side of London. The path is at its best as it passes through the Zoo. Admirers of old machinery will enjoy the locks at Hampstead Road, Kentish Town and St Pancras.

Parks Walk

The extensive parkland in Central London may come as a welcome surprise to visitors. It is possible to walk for more than an hour through a chain of parks with lakes and gardens—Victoria Embankment, St James's Park, Green Park, Hyde Park and Kensington Gardens.

7 London Country Walks

London's green belt has preserved the rural scene. A series of walks along the 330km/205mi offers a choice of a short ramble or a day-long tramp. All sections can be reached by British Rail.

❶ ROYAL LONDON

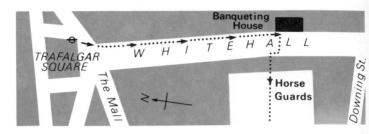

Royal London Tour

An easy tour, involving little walking, it offers the chance to see Changing the Guard on Horse Guards (1100 daily, 1000 Suns.) and at Buckingham Palace (1130 daily, alternate days in winter).

Starting from Trafalgar Sq. a short walk down Whitehall leads to the Banqueting House, the only surviving part of the old Whitehall Palace, a grandiose plan of Henry VIII. Crossing the road and passing through the Horse Guards to St James's Park, Marlborough House lies behind the trees. This was the home of Edward VII when Prince of Wales. His son, George V, was born here in 1865. Queen Alexandra made it her home after the death of her husband, Edward VII,

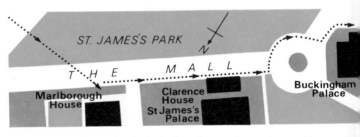

and so did Queen Mary, after the death of George V, until her own death in 1953. It is now the Commonwealth Conference Centre.

Adjacent is St James's Palace, a Tudor building, and the birthplace of Charles II, James II, Mary II, Queen Anne, and George IV. Clarence House, adjoining the palace on the south-west side, was the home of Princess Elizabeth from 1949 until she ascended the throne, and the birthplace of Princess Anne. It then became the London home of Queen Elizabeth, the Queen Mother.

Ahead is Buckingham Palace, the monarch's official residence. The Queen's

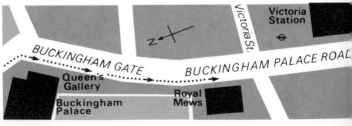

three sons, the Princes Charles, Andrew and Edward, were all born here. Passing to the left of the palace, through Buckingham Gate one comes to the entrance to the Queen's Gallery on the right, the only part of the palace open to the public. A little further on is the Royal Mews, open on Wed. and Thurs. 1400–1600 (closed Ascot Week).

The shortest way back is to continue to Victoria, then bus or Underground to Embankment or Charing Cross.

Banqueting House

St James's Palace

Buckingham Palace and Queen Victoria Memorial

State Coach in the Royal Mews

2 **CITY**

City Tour

Even though some of the places of interest are closed on Sunday, it is the best day for a sightseeing tour of the City, then almost deserted of traffic and pedestrians. Starting from St Paul's (services at 0800, 1030, 1130 and 1515) cross Cheapside to Foster Lane to see St Vedast's church, a Wren building restored after bombing in 1940. The steeple by Wren survived. Robert Herrick, the poet, was baptized in an earlier church on the site in 1591. A short walk down Cheapside takes you past the famous and beautiful Bow Bells church, St Mary Le Bow. King St., on the left, leads to the Guildhall. Along Gresham

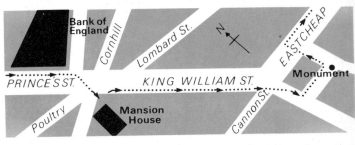

St., a right turn into Prince's St. takes you to the heart of the City, with the Bank of England and the Mansion House at the junction of six roads. King William St. leads to the Monument, commemorating the Great Fire of London. Eastcheap and Great Tower St. lead to the ancient church of All Hallows (brass rubbing weekdays May-Oct. 1000–1700), and to Tower Hill and the Tower. The most convenient way for return to Central London is from Tower Hill Underground.

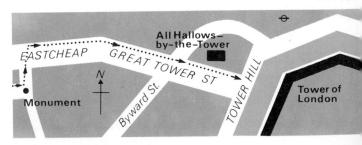

St Paul's Cathedral

The Guildhall

Tower of London

The Monument

❸ **FLOODLIGHT**

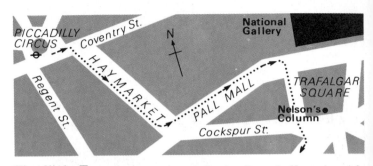

Floodlight Tour

Public buildings are floodlit from dusk to midnight. Start off in Piccadilly Circus, where commercial lights and advertising signs are the brightest and most numerous in London. Down the Haymarket a left turn into Pall Mall East brings you to Trafalgar Sq. with the National Gallery, the fountains, and Nelson's column floodlit. On the south side, in the Mall, the

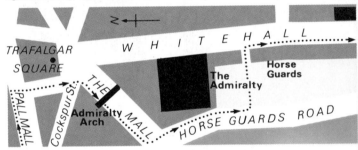

Admiralty Arch and the Admiralty building are both bathed in soft light. Bearing left, off the Mall, into Horse Guards Rd, the Horse Guards is illuminated, and, walking through on to Whitehall, Banqueting House is an imposing floodlit sight. Finally, at the south end of Whitehall is the most impressive floodlighting of all – the Clock Tower, Victoria Tower, and Terrace of the Houses of Parliament; across the road lies Westminster Abbey which is an entrancing sight even for

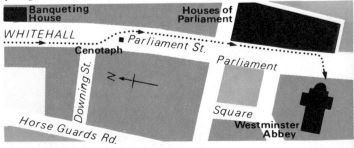

latecomers, as the floodlighting there is kept on till 0200 in the summer, two hours later than anywhere else in the city.

Trafalgar Square

Houses of Parliament

④ JUBILEE

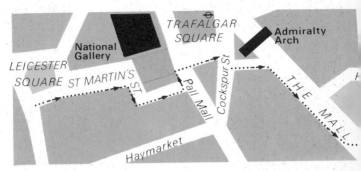

Jubilee Walkway

As London's tribute to Queen Elizabeth's Silver Jubilee, this itinerary was mapped out in 1977–8. It is in two sections – one south of the Thames and the other north. Total length is about 15km/9mi but it can, of course, be joined or left at will. The walkway passes through places old and new, enabling the visitor to gain an insight into London's past and present. Starting point is Leicester Sq. Then it runs past the Houses of Parliament, over Lambeth Bridge and along the South Bank to Southwark and Tower Bridge, the end of

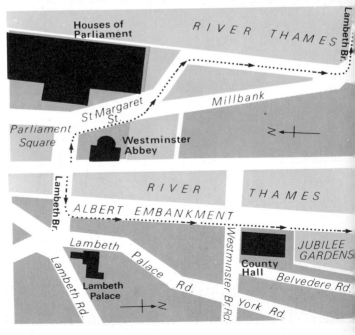

the walkway south of the Thames. The north section runs from Tower Hill, around the restored St Katharine's Docks, through the old part of the City to Mansion House and St Paul's, then through Holborn, across Kingsway to

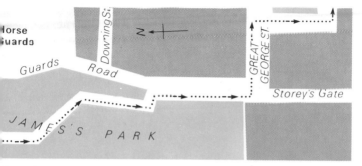

Drury Lane, Covent Garden, and finally back to the starting point in Leicester Sq.

For the greater part of the walkway little-used or completely traffic-free thoroughfares are followed. Metal disks bearing the Jubilee Crown symbol are set in the pavement at frequent intervals to serve as direction signs. A route map is also available. Apply to London Tourist Board, Victoria Station SW1.

Jubilee Walkway disk

County Hall in background

10 Downing Street

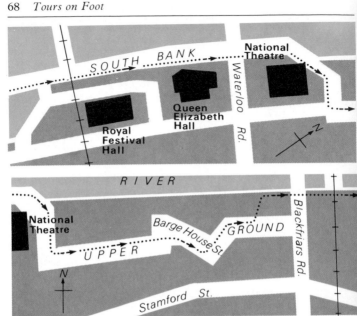

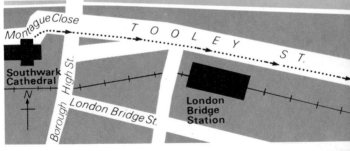

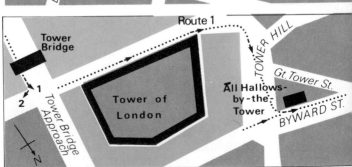

Royal Festival Hall

Southwark Cathedral

THAMES

BANKSIDE

Bankside Power Station

Southwark Br. Rd.

Clink St.

Southwark Cathedral

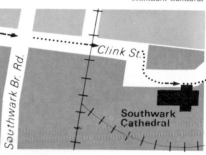

HMS Belfast

Tower Bridge

Morgan's Lane

William Curtis Ecological Park

Tooley St.

Tower Bridge Rd.

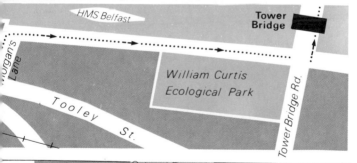

Optional **Route 2**

East Smithfield

Tower Bridge Approach

St Katharine's Dock

Thomas More St.

N

1   2   St. Katharine Way

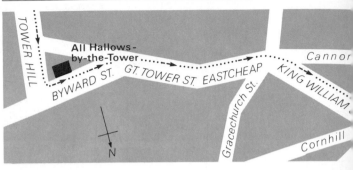

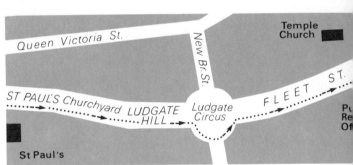

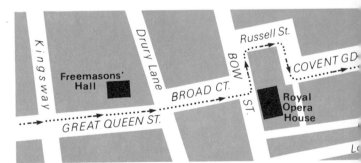

Temple Church

Royal Courts of Justice

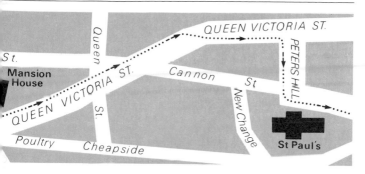

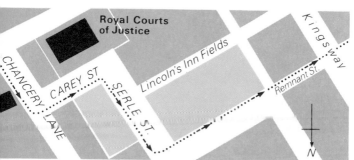

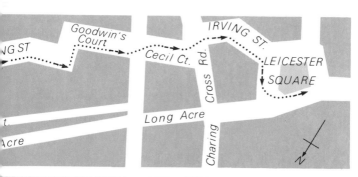

Lincoln's Inn Fields

Royal Opera House

⑤ TOWPATH

The Regent s Canal, excavated 150 years ago to enable barges to be towed between the Thames and the canal network of the rest of England, is now a peaceful backwater. A towpath walk has been laid down from the bridge at Lisson Grove W2, for a distance of about 4km/2½mi to King's Cross, providing an unusual glimpse of the north side of London.

The path can, of course, be joined or left at any of the numerous bridges. It is most attractive as it passes through Regent's Park and along the fringe of the Zoo.

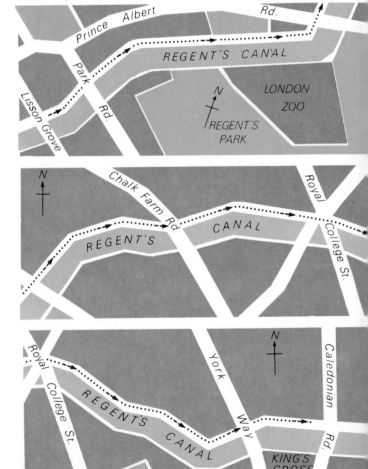

Regent's Canal at the Zoo

Hampstead Road Lock

Pleasure boat on the canal

6 PARKS

Thanks to the prevalence of open spaces, carefully tended and invariably attractive with flower beds, it is possible to stroll for more than an hour with only a few minutes beset by traffic and busy streets. The route stretches from the western edge of the City as far as Kensington though, of course, there is always an Underground station or bus stop close at hand en route.

Starting at the east end of the Strand, walk down Savoy Hill to the Thames Embankment. Gardens run alongside the road as far as Charing Cross railway bridge. Towering above the tree-shaded lawns are the Savoy Hotel and Shell Mex House with the largest clock face in London. The walk is fringed by statues, including memorials to Rabbie Burns and Sir Arthur Sullivan. At the west end, among formal flower beds, is an open-air café and a bandstand; often there is also an exhibition of amateur art.

Cross the busy road beyond the railway bridge, and a narrow grassy area extends almost as far as Westminster Bridge. Note the remains of a stone wall and a flight of steps on the right, part of a 17th-century palace built for Mary II, indicating how wide the Thames used to be.

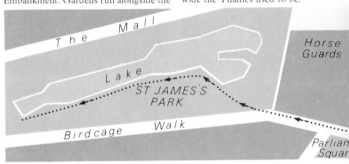

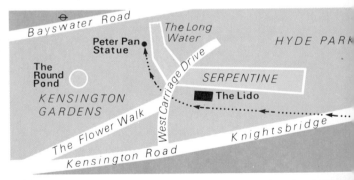

St James's Park

Rotten Row, Hyde Park

Cross Parliament Sq. to Birdcage Walk, and there is the entrance to London's most beautiful park, St James's. Just beside the lake there is a charming café, the modern version of the dairy which, a century ago, kept cows in a yard to serve fresh milk to patrons. Walk along the side of the lake, with its scores of water birds, and cross the Mall in front of Buckingham Palace. The broad walk of Green Park leads straight to Piccadilly, but by walking diagonally among the trees you emerge at Hyde Park Corner. A subway runs below this road junction to Hyde Park. The flower beds in this corner are a feature, and include a 'wild' area where rabbits hop amongst the birds.

Either side of the Serpentine is enjoyable, the south side goes past London's favourite spot for sunbathing and swimming, the Lido. Cross the West Carriage Drive and on the other side is Kensington Gardens, quieter and less frequented. Bear left and there is the Flower Walk, the traditional promenade for children's nurses and their wealthy wards; keep to the right along the water and you come to the Peter Pan statue. To the north is Bayswater Rd and to the south Kensington Rd, both of which have frequent bus services to take you back to Central London.

The distance covered is about 6km/3½mi.

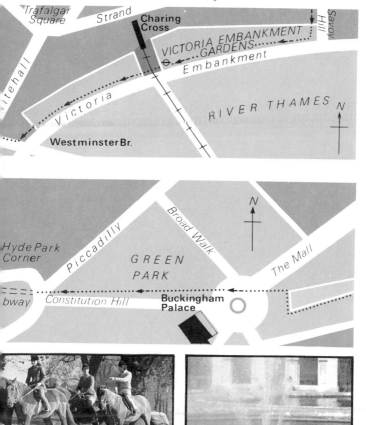

Kensington Gardens

London Country Walks

Thanks to building restrictions London's Green Belt covers a wide area around London and its suburbs. It lies beyond the M25 motorway but is easily reached by British Rail routes and by some Green Line and National Express coaches. From the BR stations and coach stops in towns and villages well-signposted footpaths, bridleways, and lanes pass through woodlands, fields and common land.

The itinerary based on the diagram below covers a series of walks totalling 330km/205mi at an average distance of 40km/25mi from the centre of London.

Distance between adjacent BR stations is about 16km/10mi, offering a start from one station and return from another.

London main line stations for these walks are: *Charing Cross* for Gravesend, Meopham, Sevenoaks; *Euston* for King's Langley; *Fenchurch St.* for Tilbury (ferry to Gravesend); *King's Cross* for Brookman's Park; *Liverpool St.* for Brentwood, Broxbourne, Epping; *Marylebone* for Great Missenden, High Wycombe; *Paddington* for Maidenhead, Windsor; *St Pancras* for St Albans; *Victoria* for Hurst Green, Mertsham; *Waterloo* for Sunningdale, Box Hill, W. Byfleet.

Thames at Windsor

Thames at Gravesend

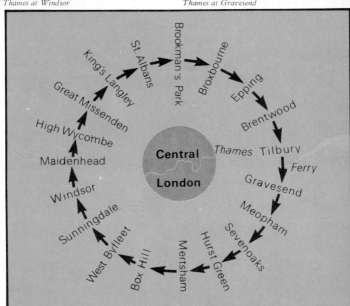

GAZETTEER

City of London coat of arms

THE CITY

This 'square mile' of London is easy to explore on foot if you start from the centre at the Mansion House (buses 6, 8, 9, 11, 15, 21, 22, 25, 43, 76, 133. Underground Bank), from which six streets radiate. In the immediate vicinity are the Bank of England, Stock Exchange, St Mary Le Bow, Temple of Mithras and London Stone. King William St. leads to the Monument and from there All Hallows church and the Tower of London are at the end of Eastcheap and Great Tower St. North from the Mansion House along Moorgate the Guildhall, Barbican and the Museum of London are on the left, and, after Moorgate becomes City Rd, Wesley's house is on the right and Bunhill Fields on the left. Back to the Mansion House, St Paul's, in its new and spacious precincts, looms among the high-rise office blocks, with the Postal Museum, St Bartholomew's Hospital and church, and Smithfield to the north. A short walk along Newgate St. leads to the Old Bailey, then down Ludgate Hill to Fleet St. with St Bride's church on the left and Dr Johnson's house and the Cheshire Cheese on the right. A little further on, the Temple is behind offices and shops on the left and on the right stands St Dunstan-in-the-West with a statue of Elizabeth I carved in 1586.

All Hallows-by-the-Tower
3N3

Tower Hill EC3 The church stands on what may be the site of the oldest religious building in London. Bombs largely destroyed it in 1940, exposing a tessellated Roman pavement. During the rebuilding a layer of ash from Boadicea's attack on the city, *ca* AD 61, was revealed, as well as an Anglo-Saxon arch and parts of two stone crosses. Many famous people have worshipped here; **William Penn** was baptized at its font in 1644, and **John Quincy Adams**, sixth President of the USA, was married before its altar.

Bank of England
3N3

Threadneedle St. EC2 The financial heart of Britain, founded in 1694, is mainly a 20th-century building, incorporating the columns and windowless walls designed by **Sir John Soane** at the end of the 18th century. The nation's gold reserves are stored in vaults guarded by electronic equipment. Only the entrance hall is open to the public (on previous application).

Barbican
3M2

EC2 This modern development, which has preserved traces of the Roman city, combines residences, two exhibition halls and a cultural complex. The last, the **Barbican Centre**, includes a concert hall, home of the London Symphony Orchestra; a theatre, base of the Royal Shakespeare Company; the Pit Theatre; three cinemas, art gallery, library and restaurants.
Buses 4, 8, 9, 11, 21, 22, 25, 43, 76. Underground Moorgate or Barbican. Coach leaves ½hr after each performance in theatre or concert hall to Charing Cross, Victoria and Waterloo stations.

Bunhill Fields
3M2

City Rd EC1 A burial ground originally used to inter the remains moved from the charnel house in St Paul's during the 16th century, it later became a **cemetery** for non-conformists. It is the resting place of many famous people, including **John Bunyan**, **Daniel Defoe**, **William Blake**, and, in the adjacent Quakers' ground, **George Fox**.

Cheshire Cheese   3L3
Wine Office Court, Fleet St. EC4 A
favourite tavern of journalists and tour-
ists, and famous for its meat puddings. It
is little altered from the days when **Dr
Johnson** and **Oliver Goldsmith** added
their names to the visitors' book.

Guildhall see p. 50

Dr Johnson's House see p. 51

Mansion House   3M3
EC4 The official residence of the **Lord
Mayor** of London was built, 1739–53, in
Palladian style. It is in the **Egyptian
Hall**, one of a series of state rooms, that
the historic banquets are held. Inspection
only by prior written application to the
Lord Mayor's secretary.

Mermaid Theatre   3L3
Puddle Dock EC4 A small modern theatre
overlooking the Thames, it was the first
theatre to be built in the City for three
centuries. It is as near as possible to the
site of a theatre which flourished from
1576 to 1653, the venue of the company of
players known as the King's Men, in
which **Shakespeare** was a stockholder.

Mithras Temple   3M3
Queen Victoria St. EC4 During excavations to lay foundations for a new office
building in 1954, the remains of a Roman
temple to Mithras, the god of light, were
uncovered. The superb sculptures discovered at the same time are on display in
the Museum of London (p. 51).

Monument   3N3
Fish St. Hill EC4 The column was designed by **Christopher Wren** to commemorate the Great Fire of London. The
height of 61.6m/202ft is reputed to be the
distance from its base to the baker's shop
where the fire began. An interior spiral
staircase of 311 steps ends in a gallery
giving a superb view of the City.

Museum of London see p. 51

Old Bailey   3L3
Newgate St. EC1 Dominated by the
bronze figure of Justice on the dome, the
Central Criminal Court stands on the
site of the notorious **Newgate jail**. The
present building was completed in 1907,
with large extensions added in the 1960s.
Most of the famous trials of murderers,
spies and other major criminals arrested in
London, the Home Counties and on the
high seas, take place here.

Postal Museum see p. 54

St Bartholomew the Great
                               3M2
Smithfield EC1 The City's oldest church.
It escaped both the Great Fire of 1666 and
the bombing of 1940–5. Originally it was a
priory built by Rahere, but there was

St Bartholomew the Great

St Paul's Cathedral

The Monument

Bronze figure of Justice, Old Bailey

Bank of England and New Stock Exchange

much rebuilding in the 16th century. During a checkered history, part of the church became a printer's shop, in which **Benjamin Franklin** worked in 1725.

St Bartholomew's Hospital
3L3

Smithfield EC1 London's oldest hospital was founded by Rahere in 1123, after he had vowed to do so if he recovered from malaria. It has been tending the sick ever since and is now one of the major teaching hospitals in the country. The hospital area is itself a parish and has a church inside the grounds.

St Brides
3L3

Fleet St. EC4 The slim spire of the church was designed by **Wren** to contrast with the massive dome of St Paul's. Mercifully it remained intact when the church was bombed. Excavations during restoration of the nave revealed traces of seven earlier churches on the site, and the finds are now housed in the crypt.

St Mary Le Bow
3M3

Cheapside EC2 The Londoners' best-loved church. To be born within earshot of its bells is to be a true London **cockney**, and the same bells allegedly beckoned **Dick Whittington** in 1397 to return to the City and become Lord Mayor. The original bells were lost in the Great Fire and, after their replacements crashed down in an air raid in 1941, the metal was retrieved and cast into the present bells.

St Paul's
3M3

Ludgate Hill EC4 The hill on which the **cathedral** stands is believed to have been the site of a pagan temple. A wooden Christian church stood there by the 7th century, soon replaced by a stone building in 675–85. Viking raiders demolished it, and another building rising on the ruins was destroyed by fire in 1087. The new church was not completed until 1287. It had the tallest spire and was claimed to be the largest religious building in Europe. Its fabric gradually deteriorated and the Great Fire hastened its end in 1666. The present cathedral, masterpiece of **Wren**, was begun in 1675 and completed in 1710.

The style is a unique blend of Gothic and Renaissance architecture with an early baroque interior. The high altar was destroyed during air raids; the present one is based on Wren's design and is dedicated to the Commonwealth war dead. Behind it is the memorial chapel to the dead of the US forces. Within the great dome is the famous **Whispering Gallery** and around its exterior the Stone and Golden Galleries giving superb views of the City. In the crypt, among the largest of any church in the world, are memorials to many illustrious dead, including **Nelson** and

Wellington. A simple marble slab marks the resting place of Wren with the inscription (in Latin) *if you seek a memorial, look around*, composed by his son.

Stock Exchange see p. 56

Temple   3K3

EC4 Approached from Fleet St., the Embankment or, better still, through Wren's original gatehouse in Middle Temple Lane, this is an area of peace and tranquillity – much as it has been since the 17th century, thanks to careful restoration of war damage. Originally the property of the Knights Templars, military champions during the Crusades, and of the Knights Hospitallers of St John who succeeded them, the Temple has been the centre of England's legal community for seven centuries. **Middle Temple Hall** is a magnificent Tudor building with a serving table made of timber from Francis Drake's *Golden Hind*, beautiful Elizabethan carvings, and glowing heraldic glass. Shakespeare's own players performed *Twelfth Night* in this hall in 1602. The **Temple Church** is one of the few round churches in England.

Tower Hill   3O3

EC3 A time-honoured place for public meetings and political rallies, as it still is at lunchtime from Monday to Friday. It is also the place where traitors and political criminals were hanged, beheaded, or drawn and quartered. A small area in **Trinity Gardens** marks the spot where so many guilty, and innocent, were put to death. In front of the gardens is the double memorial to the 38,000 men of the mercantile navy and fishing fleets who died in two world wars.

Tower of London   3O3

EC3 William the Conqueror built the White Tower as a precaution against sudden attacks from the vanquished Londoners. Monarch after monarch added to the original and the Tower has served as a palace, prison, royal treasury, mint, observatory, even a zoo. Its awesome history of treason, intrigue, injustice, and torture lingers at every turn – the **Traitor's Gate** at the edge of the river; the **Bloody Tower** where tradition says the Little Princes, Edward V and his brother the Duke of York, were murdered and Sir Walter Raleigh was imprisoned for a year; the **White Tower** with its torture chamber. The **Jewel House** with its priceless treasures of the royal regalia, and the surrounding grounds, where the tame ravens and the Yeoman Warders (also known as Beefeaters) in their Tudor uniform, provide a contrast to the grim yet fascinating interior. (Weekdays 0930–1700 Mar. to Oct., 0930–1600 Nov. to

Tower Bridge and Tower of London

Buckingham Palace

Feb.; Sundays 1400–1700 Mar. to Oct., closed Nov. to Feb.)

Wesley's House and Chapel
see p. 57

WESTMINSTER & WHITEHALL

The area, heart of Britain's government, forms a rough triangle easily toured on foot. From the vantage point of Trafalgar Sq. – a plaque in the pavement behind the equestrian statue of Charles I on the south side of the square marks the exact centre of London – the broad vista of Whitehall runs past the Banqueting House, the Horse Guards, Cenotaph, and the offices of Government Ministries as far as the Houses of Parliament. At the north end the Admiralty Arch stands on he right and beyond the Horse Guards is Downing St. Around Parliament Sq. are the Houses of Parliament, Westminster Abbey and St Margaret's; statues in the square include Sir Winston Churchill and Abraham Lincoln. A short distance past the Abbey, along Victoria St., a spacious piazza fronts Westminster Cathedral. Streets on the opposite side lead to Birdcage Walk and St James's Park, bounded by the Mall. Across the Mall is St James's Palace and to the left the Queen Victoria Memorial and Buckingham Palace. Returning along the Mall leads back to Trafalgar Sq.

Banqueting House   5J4
Whitehall SW1 This architectural masterpiece of **Inigo Jones** was completed in 1622 on the site of an earlier banqueting hall, destroyed by fire in 1619. The design was inspired by the work of the Italian architect Andrea Palladio, and the House was intended to turn **Whitehall Palace** into a magnificent and fitting royal residence. But the buildings already in existence were burned down in yet another fire in 1698, and Whitehall was never again a royal palace, though the Banqueting House remains to give a hint of what might have been. Above the entrance is a bust of **Charles I**, marking the site of the window through which the king stepped to reach the scaffold in Whitehall for his execution. The weather vane on the roof was put there on the orders of **James II** to warn him when the wind was favourable for the fleet of William of Orange to sail from Holland. Presumably in November 1688 the vane indicated the ominous east wind, and the king had ultimately to flee to France. The interior of the main hall, restored in 1973 to its original design, is memorable for its vast size and the nine allegorical ceiling paintings by **Rubens** and his pupils.

Buses 3, 11, 12, 24, 29, 39, 53, 59, 77, 88. Underground Charing Cross.

terior of Banqueting House

Buckingham Palace   5H4

SW1 The home of the sovereign in the capital (the Royal Standard is flown when the Queen is in residence) was originally the 18th-century London seat of the Duke of Buckingham. It was bought by **George III** for his consort Queen Charlotte, and was then called the Queen's House. **George IV** ordered alterations and extensions but never lived in it. **Queen Victoria** was the first monarch to make it the permanent residence of the Court. It is the rear of the palace which is seen from the Mall, the real front overlooks the palace gardens. The **State Apartments** are notably the Throne Room, the State Ballroom and the Picture Gallery, not open to the general public, but used for investitures, formal banquets and receptions. The royal family's private apartments are in the north wing. The ceremony of **Changing the Guard** takes place daily at 1130 (alternate mornings in winter; not held in bad weather). (No buses in the Mall, nearest as for Trafalgar Sq. or Pall Mall.)
Underground Charing Cross, Green Park or Hyde Park Corner.

Canada House   5J4

Trafalgar Square SW1 The HQ of the High Commissioner for Canada was built in the early 19th century and rebuilt in 1925. Facilities for Canadian visitors include an information bureau.
(Transport as for Trafalgar Sq.)

Cenotaph   5J4

Whitehall SW1 The war memorial, designed by **Sir Edward Lutyens**, was erected in 1920. The inscription is simply 'To Our Glorious Dead', with no reference to creed, denomination or nationality of those servicemen who died during World War I. A second inscription was added to honour the dead of World War II. On the Sunday nearest to 11 November a memorial service is held, attended by the royal family, government representatives and members of the armed services.
Buses 3, 11, 12, 24, 29, 39, 53, 59, 76, 77, 88. Underground Charing Cross or Westminster.

Duke of York's Column

The Mall SW1 The column is topped by a bronze statue to honour the son of George III who was C-in-C of the British Army in 1798. His dubious martial qualities are immortalized in the rhyme about his marching his troops up a hill and down again. The Duke's unpopularity was only increased when every soldier in the army had one day's pay stopped to help pay for the column.
(Transport as for Trafalgar Sq.)

Life Guard on sentry duty in Whitehall

Clock Tower of the Houses of Parliament

Guards' Chapel

Birdcage Walk SW1 The place of worship for the Household Cavalry and the regiment of Foot Guards lies within the grounds of **Wellington Barracks**. The chapel was hit by a flying bomb one Sunday in June 1944 while a service was in progress, killing 121 people. Parts of the chapel which were retrieved have been incorporated in the new and beautiful building. The choir at the Sunday services is accompanied by a Guards' band (tickets of admission are allocated by the chaplain).

(No buses, nearest as for Westminster Cathedral.)

Horse Guards   5J4

Whitehall SW1 The two Horse Guards who remain immobile on their mounts, each for one hour of sentry duty between 1000 to 1600, are posted under arches which were originally part of the guard-house of the old **Whitehall Palace**. Changing the Guard ceremony takes place 1100 (weekdays) 1000 (Sun.). Beyond the buildings behind the sentries is Horse Guards Parade, used for the ceremony of **Trooping the Colour** in June.

(Transport as for Trafalgar Sq.)

Houses of Parliament   5J4

SW1 Officially known as the New Palace of Westminster, the Houses of Parliament still rank as a royal palace. The original **Palace of Westminster** was the residence of the sovereign from the 11th to the 15th centuries, first becoming the seat of Parliament in 1547. The present buildings replaced the old palace, almost completely destroyed by fire in 1834. Work began in 1836 and was not completed until 1888, though both the Lords and Commons were meeting in the new chambers in the 1850s. The **Victoria Tower**, at the south-west corner, the tallest square tower in the world, rises 103m/336ft and is the repository for Parliamentary records. This part is occupied by the **House of Lords**. The debating chamber is an elaborately decorated Gothic hall, with a dais on which is the Queen's throne. In front of it is the Woolsack, since the 14th century a symbol of England's prosperity through the wool trade.

The north-east end is dominated by the clock tower (97m/320ft), with the famous bell **Big Ben**, weighing more than 13½ tons, cast in 1858. The clock is famous for its accuracy.

The **House of Commons**, almost destroyed in May 1941, has been rebuilt in Gothic style with many contributions from the Commonwealth – including the Speaker's chair from Australia, the table

Duke of York's Column

from Canada, the clerks' chairs from South Africa (at the time in the Commonwealth), the dispatch boxes from New Zealand.

Between the two Palace Yards which give access to the Lords and the Commons is **Westminster Hall**, to the left of St Stephen's entrance. It is undoubtedly the finest secular building of its kind in the world. Originally built in the 11th century, it was rebuilt three centuries later. Time, fire and war have not been allowed to mar its magnificence. Stairs at one corner lead to **St Stephen's Crypt**, in which is a chapel where Members of Parliament, irrespective of sect, may arrange their weddings and have their children christened.

Public admission to the Houses of Parliament with or without a guide was suspended for security reasons in 1981. For latest information contact London Tourist Board, Information Centre, Victoria Station SW1 (tel. 730 3488).

The **galleries**, where visitors listen to debates, have restricted accommodation and permits from an MP or official must always be obtained. Overseas visitors will find it simplest to apply to their embassy or consulate for the appropriate introduction.
Buses 3, 11, 12, 24, 29, 39, 53, 59, 76, 77, 88. Underground Westminster.

Leicester Square   2J3

WC2 Laid out three centuries ago, this traffic-free square was originally a lonely area just north of the houses of Westminster and a favourite resort of duellists, footpads and vagrants. In 1874 it was turned into a formal garden with a literary flavour typified by the statue of Shakespeare in the centre. The busts on the fringes of the garden commemorate famous local residents: the artists **Hogarth** and **Reynolds**; **John Hunter**, the founder of surgical pathology, and **Sir Isaac Newton**, discoverer of the law of gravitation. Today the square has been largely given over to food and entertainment. In the north-east corner is the church of **Notre Dame**, the London church of the French, built a century ago but bombed in 1940. The present building is a fine example of modern religious architecture. Inside are murals by **Jean Cocteau** and a superb Aubusson tapestry above the altar.
Buses 1, 24, 29. Underground Leicester Sq.

Mall, The   5H4

SW1 The impressive boulevard, stretching from the Admiralty Arch (erected in memory of Queen Victoria in 1910) to the Queen Victoria Memorial, was first laid down during the reign of Charles II.

Queen Victoria Memorial

Carlton House Terrace, the Mall

Changing the Guard, St James's Palace

It was given its present tree-lined appearance in 1911.
(No buses or Underground, nearest as for Trafalgar Sq.)

New Zealand House 5J4
Haymarket SW1 The HQ of the High Commissioner for New Zealand, completed in 1963, has information rooms, library and facilities for visitors from New Zealand. The tower (not open to the public) is 69m/225ft high.
Buses 1, 3, 6, 9, 11, 12, 13, 15, 24, 29, 39, 53, 59. Underground Piccadilly Circus.

Pall Mall 5H4
SW1 This wide street runs from the end of Haymarket to the private road serving St James's Palace. The name comes from an old French version of the game of croquet, called paille maille, played on this level ground during the reign of Charles II. Many of London's most exclusive clubs are in this street, the first in London to be illuminated by gas (1807). Among famous residents in the past were **Nell Gwyn** and the artist **Gainsborough**.
Buses 3, 6, 9, 12, 13, 15, 53, 59, 88. Underground Piccadilly Circus.

Queen Victoria Memorial 5H4
SW1 Often regarded as unduly fussy and spoiling the vista of Buckingham Palace, approaching from the Mall, this large memorial of 1911, designed by **Aston Webb** and sculpted by **Thomas Brock**, manages to symbolize all that was good about the old Queen and her reign. Her statue is 4m/13ft high, carved from white marble, and is surrounded by groups representing Justice, Truth and Mother hood. The groups in bronze symbolize Science & Art, Peace & Progress, Naval & Military Power, Industry & Agriculture. On the balustrade are the heraldic shields of the nations of the British Commonwealth.
(No buses or Underground, nearest as for Trafalgar Sq. or Pall Mall.)

St James's Palace 5H4
Pall Mall SW1 St James's Palace is the best example of a brick-built mansion of Tudor London (no admission to interior). The name is taken from an old leper hospital dedicated to St James the Less. **Henry VIII** built a palace on the site, probably to a plan drawn up by Holbein, but continued to prefer the spaciousness of Whitehall Palace, as did his successors until it was destroyed by fire in 1698. St James's then became the London residence of the monarch until the reign of Victoria. It is still regarded as the traditional home of the ruling house, and ambassadors to Britain are accredited to

the **Court of St James's**. The gatehouse is the best preserved relic of the Tudor building. The much-altered **Chapel Royal**, on the east side, has a magnificent painted ceiling. At the Sunday services (visitors admitted) the choristers wear Tudor costume.
(Buses and Underground as for Pall Mall)

St Margaret's 5J4

Parliament Sq. SW1 The parish church of the **House of Commons** has a pew allocated to the Speaker for occasions when MPs attend formally. It was built in the 16th century, replacing a much earlier church, and has been twice restored. Some of the stained glass windows are of particular interest: the east window is Flemish glass of the early 15th century; beside the south aisle the windows are the work of **John Piper** and were installed in 1967. The church has long been the choice for the weddings of prominent persons – from **Samuel Pepys** in 1655 to **Sir Winston Churchill** in 1908. A stone on the exterior of the church is a memorial to leaders of the Commonwealth Parliament who were directly or indirectly responsible for the arrest of Charles I and whose corpses were thrown into a common grave by command of Charles II after the Restoration in 1660. **Sir Walter Raleigh's** body is also believed to have been buried in the floor of the church after his execution. He has a commemorative window, a gift from the USA.
(Buses and Underground as for Houses of Parliament)

St Martin-in-the-Fields 5J4

Trafalgar Sq. WC2 Gardens and farmland existed around the site of the present church in medieval times, and the monks from Westminster who worked there built themselves a chapel, probably as early as 1150. Henry VIII approved a larger church, and this in turn was replaced. In 1726 the present Grecian-style church was completed, the finest work of **James Gibbs** who had been taught his craft by Wren. The splendid ceiling (recently restored) above the nave is the work of Italian decorators. The large crypt, with vaults once used for the burial of hundreds of local inhabitants (including **Nell Gwyn**), has since been a refuge for the homeless, a resting place for soldiers on leave in two world wars, and an air raid shelter. Over 50 organizations devoted to charity, music, drama, and so on, now use it as a meeting place. St Martin's is the parish church of the **sovereign** and of the **Admiralty**, and by tradition it is used for memorial services for distinguished **authors** and **actors**. Of interest to Americans is the registry entry of the marriage

St Martin's in the Fields, Trafalgar Square

Westminster Abbey

of **Benjamin West**, the artist born in Springfield, Pa., who settled in London in 1763 and became President of the Royal Academy.
(Buses and Underground as for Trafalgar Sq.)

South Africa House

Trafalgar Sq, WC2 Completed in 1933, the exterior bears sculptures portraying animals and plants of the republic, dominated by a bronze winged springbok. Inside is a large British-woven tapestry showing a map of the country. The building is also the Embassy.
(Buses and Underground as for Trafalgar Sq.)

Trafalgar Square   5J4

WC2 Most of this large space was occupied by the Royal Mews until 1829, when clearance began in order to lay out a square in honour of Nelson. His monument, **Nelson's column**, is 51.2m 167ft 6in. high and the figure of Britain's naval hero on the top measures 5.3m 17ft 4½in. The bronze reliefs on the pedestal, showing scenes from the battles of the Nile, Cape St Vincent, Copenhagen and Trafalgar, were cast from captured French cannon. The four lions crouching at the base of the column are the work of **Sir Edwin Landseer** and were cast in 1868 from cannon retrieved from the sunken *Royal George*, which capsized in Portsmouth harbour in 1782 with several hundred casualties. The monument is decorated annually on 21 October, the anniversary of the Battle of Trafalgar. The square is a traditional centre for political meetings and demonstrations, usually on Sunday afternoons. And every December a giant Christmas tree given by Norway is erected in the square.
Buses 1, 3, 6, 9, 11, 12, 13, 15, 24, 29, 39, 53, 59, 77, 88. Underground Charing Cross.

Westminster Abbey   5J5

SW1 Superb in architecture, the Abbey is unsurpassed as a treasure-house of past glory, and as the inspiration of Christianity over a span of more than a thousand years. Tradition has it that the first church was in existence by AD 616. About a century later Benedictine monks founded a monastery (minster) west of the walled city of London. The name, soon adopted, of Westminster suggests that another minster lay east of the city.

A year before the Norman Conquest of 1066, a large abbey had been consecrated. Its founder, **Edward the Confessor**, was mortally ill and unable to attend the ceremony. His body was laid to rest behind the altar, where it still remains.

Henry III decided to rebuild in homage

to Edward, who had been canonized in 1161. Much of the construction was completed before Henry died in 1272. Further additions and rebuilding took place in 1376, 1388, 1441, 1503 and 1519. Restoration and minor additions have been continued ever since.

Enter by the west door and take in the glorious Gothic **nave**, 30.6m/102ft high, stretching towards the Choir, Altar Sanctuary, and Edward the Confessor's Chapel. Immediately beyond the doorway is the grave of the **Unknown Warrior**, whose body was brought from France in 1920. It lies in earth from all the battlefields of the Western Front, under a slab of Belgian marble. On the adjacent pillar is the Congressional Medal of Honour awarded by the USA. Close to the grave is a memorial stone to Sir Winston Churchill.

On the right is **St George's Chapel**, dedicated to the dead of World War I and the civilians killed in World War II. Floor slabs mark the graves of British Generals of World War I and there is a memorial tablet to President **Franklin Roosevelt**. American visitors will also be interested in a memorial stone in the nave near the chapel. It marks the original grave of **George Peabody**, the only US citizen to have been buried in the Abbey. This great 19th-century philanthropist now rests in Massachusetts. Another memorial of American interest stands in the third bay of the south aisle. It is to **John André** who, after negotiating with General Benedict Arnold, was captured, sent to General Washington, tried, and hanged as a spy. The memorial's bas-relief shows Washington receiving André's petition for a dignified end as a soldier.

Moving along to the central area below the Lantern (repaired after bombing in 1941), the rose windows to left and right in the transepts transmit suffused light on the **Sanctuary**, familiar to TV audiences who watched the Queen's Coronation in 1953. In the south transept is **Poets' Corner**, with tombs or memorials to writers and actors. The names commemorate most authors who have added lustre to works in the English language – Chaucer, Edmund Spenser, Browning, Tennyson, Longfellow, Keats, Shelley, Byron, and, of course, Shakespeare. The roll of honour runs to scores of names.

Returning to the nave, passing the Sanctuary, the visitor comes to the most sacred spot in the Abbey, **St Edward's Chapel**, with the shrine of marble over the saint's body. This is the site of the main part of the original Saxon church and has been a place of pilgrimage for nearly a thousand years. At the sides of the

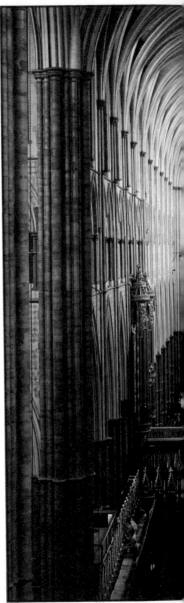

Interior of Westminster Abbey

chapel are tombs of kings and queens, the most splendid being that of Henry III, founder of the Abbey. Here also is the Coronation Chair, carved in oak for Edward I in the 13th century, and below the seat the Stone of Scone, used for the coronations of Scottish kings from the 9th century until it was brought to Westminster in 1297 as a symbol of the subjugation of Scotland by Edward I, the 'hammer of the Scots'. This warrior king is buried in the chapel. His tomb was opened about two centuries ago and the corpse measured, showing he was a man 1.9m/6ft 2in tall.

Further on, reached by a flight of steps, is the **Henry VII Chapel**, its lace-like stonework a masterpiece of late Gothic art. Gorgeous colour is added by the banners of the Knights of the Bath, the order of chivalry founded in 1399, whose chapel this is. There are more tombs of kings and queens here. The subsidiary chapel at the far end is dedicated to the RAF, with a stained glass window displaying the badges of the fighter squadrons which took part in the Battle of Britain. Note the hole in the stonework: it was caused by a wartime bomb and has been deliberately left unrepaired.

Two aisles run along each side of the chapel. On the left is the tomb of Elizabeth I and her sister Mary, buried together. A small sculptured coffin contains the remains of the little princes, sons of Edward IV, put to death in the Tower in 1483. The aisle on the right has the impressive tomb of Mary, Queen of Scots; her body was brought from its original grave by her son, James I.

If time is limited the most rewarding part to visit next is the **Chapter House** on the right, the birthplace of the parliamentary system of government, for here the Great Council first met in 1257, followed by Parliament until 1547, when it moved to the Palace of Westminster. Appropriately, the link between this site of democratic freedom and New World democracy is symbolized by two memorial tablets to US statesmen who worked in Britain – James R. Lowell, US Minister in London from 1880–5, and Walter Page, US Ambassador during the First World War.

Next to the Chapter House is the **Chamber of the Pyx**, at first a chapel (the altar here is the oldest in the Abbey) and then put to secular use as a strongroom for the pyx, or chest, containing gold and silver coins against which the purity and value of the coins of the realm were measured. (By the reign of Edward III the Barons of the Exchequer had to make the test every three months.)

Beyond this chamber is the **Norman Undercroft**. The only surviving part of the church built by Edward the Confessor before the rebuilding in 1245, it has been adapted as a museum. Of special interest are the wax or wooden effigies of kings and queens carried, as was the custom, in the funeral procession. These effigies were accurate, rather than idealized, portrayals and they show the appearance in old age of monarchs such as Edward III, Henry VII, Elizabeth I and Charles II.

(Buses and Underground as for Houses of Parliament)

Westminster Cathedral 5H5

Ashley Place SW1 The buildings along Victoria St. which obscured the magnificent front of the cathedral have been removed, and a spacious square lets one appreciate the impressive proportions of this modern addition to the religious buildings of London. The cathedral is the seat of the Archbishop of Westminster, and the most important Catholic church in the country. The foundation stone was laid in 1895. It was consecrated in 1910, though it had been used for services seven years earlier.

The style is early Byzantine, reminiscent of cathedrals in Florence, Venice and Istanbul, and the alternate bands of red brick and white stone are unique in English church architecture.

Passing through the main doorway, above which is a mosaic of Christ in Majesty, one sees the huge **nave**, 46m/150ft wide, including the side chapels. The columns and piers in dark red granite and green and white marble take the eye upwards to the great **dome** rising to 36m/117ft above the floor. The stations of the Cross on the fourteen main piers are by **Eric Gill**. At the end of the nave is a statue of St Peter, a replica of that in the Vatican.

The baptistery altar was presented by the Royal Canadian Air Force as a memorial to the airmen who died in World War II. **St Patrick's Chapel** has badges of Irish regiments who fought in World War I. Scotland has its own **St Andrew's Chapel**. From the sacristy, visitors who have obtained prior permission may visit the **crypt** containing religious relics, including pieces of the True Cross.

The sanctuary, raised above the floor of the nave, has a large altar of English granite and remains covered except on Good Friday.

An elevator goes to the **campanile**, 83m/273ft high, surmounted by a tall crucifix (1030–1700, tickets at entrance); the view from the top is impressive.

(Buses 11, 24, 29, 39. Underground St James's Park or Victoria.

Interior of Westminster Cathedral

Piccadilly Circus

WEST END & MAYFAIR

The most popular area for entertainment and shopping. Piccadilly Circus makes a good starting place. From there you can choose from Soho to the north, Regent St. curving away north west, and Piccadilly running south west, with Bond St. halfway down on the right. From the top of Regent St., Oxford St. runs east and west, with, at the west end, Marble Arch at the corner of Hyde Park. Park Lane runs south along the edge of Hyde Park as far as Hyde Park Corner, where it joins Piccadilly. From there within easy walking distance, along the south edge of Hyde Park, are Knightsbridge and Brompton Rd.

Albany

Piccadilly W1 Discreetly isolated by a courtyard, apartments occupy an 18th-century mansion converted in 1802 into 'residential chambers for bachelor gentlemen'. They have been the London homes of generations of famous men, including **Lord Byron, Lord Macaulay** and **William Gladstone**. They are not open to the public.
Buses 3, 6, 9, 12, 13, 14, 15, 19, 22, 38, 59, 88. Underground Piccadilly Circus or Green Park.

All Souls Church　　　2G3

Langham Place W1 Partially hidden by an office block and Broadcasting House, defeating the intention of the architect **John Nash** that the church's classic front and slim spire should be seen from the main section of Regent St., All Souls has an interesting interior now completely modernized. Many of the BBC's religious services are transmitted from the church, and there is a radio studio in the crypt.
Buses 3, 6, 7, 8, 12, 13, 15, 25, 39, 53, 59, 73, 88. Underground Oxford Circus.

Baker Street　　　1F2

W1 This attractive thoroughfare, running north from Oxford St., was built at the end of the 18th century with spacious residences on either side. Its fame has come from fiction: the street in which **Sherlock Holmes** lived. The location of his apartment, described by Conan Doyle as 221b, is a topic for argument among devotees. Its most feasible site is occupied by the offices of a building society just north of Marylebone Rd.
Buses 1, 2, 13, 18, 27, 30, 59, 74. Underground Baker St.

Berkeley Square　　　2G3

W1 A tree-filled square (the plane trees are mostly more than 170 years old) developed from the park surrounding a mansion, owned by the Duke of Devonshire, in 1747. Thereafter the residents were among the wealthiest in

Berkeley Square

London. A few of the original 18th-century houses survive, occupied as prestige offices by major companies. The garden in the centre is said to be haunted by the ghost of **Lord Clive**, founder of the British possession of India, who committed suicide in 1744 in his home at No. 45.

Buses 9, 14, 19, 22, 25, 38. Underground Bond St. or Green Park.

Bond Street   2G3, 5H4

W1 Bond St., actually two streets, New and Old Bond St., is the centre of London's finest shops for fashion, jewellery and paintings. **Sotheby's**, the famous auctioneers, are at 34 New Bond St., as they have been since 1744. A modern contrast is the Time-Life Building completed in 1952. The carvings on the balustrade are by **Henry Moore**.

Buses 6, 7, 8, 9, 12, 13, 14, 15, 19, 22, 25, 38, 59, 73, 88. Underground Bond St. or Green Park.

Broadcasting House   2G2

Portland Place W1 The HQ of the BBC, completed in 1931, with later extensions. **Eric Gill** sculpted the figures of Prospero and Ariel above the main entrance.

Buses 3, 6, 7, 8, 12, 13, 15, 25, 53, 59, 73, 88. Underground Oxford Circus.

Brompton Road   5F5

SW1 This wide thoroughfare is always busy with overseas visitors, attracted by the restaurants but especially by **Harrods**, the world-famous store which dominates the road. At No. 70 is the HQ of the Independent Broadcasting Authority, with guided tours Mon.-Fri. 1000, 1330, 1430, 1530 (advance booking essential).

Buses 9, 14, 19, 22, 30, 52, 73, 74. Underground Knightsbridge.

Burlington Arcade   5H4

Piccadilly W1 Those familiar with modern shopping precincts will be interested in this early version, opened in 1819 as the result of an idea of Lord George Cavendish, with 72 shops carefully selected as regards merchandise and the status of the owners. Entry to the covered arcade is supervised by beadles who ensure that the behaviour of visitors is quiet and seemly.

Buses 9, 14, 19, 22, 38. Underground Green Park or Piccadilly Circus.

Grosvenor Square   2G3

W1 A spacious area, laid out from fields and private estates in the 18th century, now regarded as 'the US in UK'. **John Adams**, second President of the USA, lived at No. 9 after he was appointed ambassador to Britain in 1785. **General Eisenhower** established his HQ at No. 20 when he became Commanding General, European Theatre of Operations, in

Burlington Arcade, beadle in attendance

American Embassy, Grosvenor Square

1943. The impressive **US Embassy** filling the west side of the square was built in 1960. The American eagle above the entrance has a wing span of 10.7m/35ft. The statue of President **Franklin Roosevelt** in the centre of the square, the work of Sir William Reid Dick, was unveiled in 1948 by Mrs Roosevelt.

Buses 6, 7, 8, 12, 13, 15, 59, 73, 88. Underground Bond St. or Marble Arch.

Hyde Park Barracks 5F4

Knightsbridge SW1 This tower block, completed in 1970, was criticized as too large and too austere for the environment, but time has eased objections. The **Household Cavalry**, personal bodyguard of the sovereign, is stationed here, and you can see the cavalrymen setting out each morning for duty in Whitehall, or exercising their mounts in Rotten Row nearby.

Buses 9, 14, 22, 30, 52, 73, 74. Underground Knightsbridge.

Hyde Park Corner 5G4

SW1 Although an underpass now takes most of the east and west traffic, this is the busiest intersection in London; fortunately pedestrians can use subways to cross the roads. The **Wellington Arch** in the centre was erected in 1828 to honour the victor of Waterloo; Peace rides in the chariot on the top of the arch. A statue of Wellington stands on the nearby traffic island. He is surrounded by four of his soldiers, members of English, Welsh, Scottish and Irish regiments. Yet another monument to the Iron Duke's memory stands just inside the gates to the Park. Usually described as the **Achilles Statue**, it is in fact a copy of a Roman portrayal of a horse-tamer. The statue was a gift from the women of Britain to their hero and his comrades, and the metal used came from captured French cannon.

Buses 2, 9, 14, 16, 19, 22, 25, 26, 30, 36, 38, 52, 73, 74. Underground Hyde Park Corner.

Marble Arch 1F3

W1 But for a technical error when **John Nash** prepared his design, by command of George IV in 1828, this triumphal arch would have stood as the gateway to Buckingham Palace. Belatedly it was realized that the archway would be too narrow for the State Coach, and so it was moved to its present position. Nash was inspired by the Arch of Constantine near the Colosseum in Rome. North west of the arch, on the pedestrian island surrounded by streams of traffic, is a stone marking the place where **Tyburn Tree** – a gallows – stood from 1571 to 1783; and Tyburn was a place of execution for three centuries before that. Hundreds of criminals were

Officer of the Royal Horse Guards

hanged there – highwaymen, thieves, murderers, traitors and many religious martyrs.

Buses 2, 6, 7, 8, 12, 15, 16, 26, 30, 36, 73, 74, 88. Underground Marble Arch.

Oxford Street 2H3

W1 The highway, named after the 18th-century Earl of Oxford, whose estates lay to the north of the road which led from Newgate prison to Tyburn, rapidly became a popular street of shops, including, in the 19th century, the first store selling a variety of goods under one roof. Today it probably has the greatest sales turnover of any comparable area in the country. The largest store in London led the way when an American businessman, **Gordon Selfridge**, opened its doors in 1909. The street is now attractive to pedestrians as only buses and cabs are allowed for most of its length.

Buses 6, 7, 8, 12, 13, 15, 59, 73, 88. Underground Bond St., Marble Arch, Oxford Circus or Tottenham Ct Rd.

Park Lane 1F3

W1 This street, overlooking the east side of Hyde Park, was long regarded as boasting the most luxurious and costly residences in London. Now the majority of the mansions have been replaced by apartment blocks and hotels, notably the **Dorchester, Grosvenor House**, and at the south end the **London Hilton** with 24 storeys reaching a height of 91m/300ft.

Buses 2, 16, 26, 30, 36, 73, 74. Underground Hyde Park Corner or Marble Arch.

Piccadilly Circus and 2H3
Piccadilly 5H4

W1 The unusual name is derived from 'piccadill', an ornate collar combined with a cravat, worn by dandies in the 17th century. The best-known piccadill maker gained a minor fortune and built a house on the north side of the present Circus. In recent years this 'centre of the world' has been subject to various experiments to maintain traffic flow and give pedestrians access to the centre around the statue known as **Eros**. In fact the figure, erected in 1893, represents the Angel of Christian Charity, and is a memorial to the **Earl of Shaftesbury**, a Victorian philanthropist. On the north side of the Circus is the **London Experience** in the Trocadero Centre, with a multi-screen show of old and modern London. Performance every 40 minutes. 1020–2200 daily. West from the Circus, Piccadilly runs for 1.6km/1mi to Hyde Park Corner, and is a thoroughfare of high-class shops, airline offices, and, on the north side, the **Royal Academy** in Burlington House (p. 48). Buses 3, 6, 9, 12, 13, 14, 15, 19, 22, 38, 53,

Regent Street

Piccadilly pub

59, 88. Underground Piccadilly Circus or Green Park.

Regent Street 2H3

W1 The phenomenally active **John Nash**, whose work was responsible for so many of the Regency buildings in London (and Brighton), laid out this street between 1813 and 1825 at the request of his great friend, the **Prince Regent** (later George IV), because his royal highness wished for an easy route from his house near Buckingham Palace to his newly acquired Regent's Park. Rebuilding over the years has largely destroyed the splendid vistas Nash provided, but the sweeping curve just beyond Piccadilly Circus and the buildings on the right give some idea of past glory. Today it is a street of high-class shops and travel offices.

Buses 3, 6, 12, 13, 15, 39, 53, 59, 88. Underground Oxford Circus or Piccadilly Circus.

St James's Church 5H4

Piccadilly W1 One of the few **Wren** churches outside the City, severely damaged by incendiary bombs in 1940, St James's has been patiently and successfully restored. From the 18th century onwards this was the most fashionable church for baptisms and marriages in the West End, and its incumbents invariably went on to high office in the Church; three of them became archbishops. Some of the original parts of the interior were salvaged after air-raid damage, including the **Grinling Gibbon** altarpiece and the 17th-century organ. The pretty little garden, replacing the old churchyard, is to commemorate the bravery of London's civilian population during World War II. Instruction on brass rubbing Mon.-Sat. 1000–1800; Sun. 1200–1800.

(Buses and Underground as for Piccadilly)

Shepherd Market 5G4

W1 Easily missed by visitors, this area of narrow twisting lanes and passages can be reached from the south end of Park Lane or the west end of Piccadilly. This is the real **May Fair**; here in the 17th century and early 18th century, 1 May was celebrated by local people who still retained their memories of rural life. Gradually it became a year-round amusement centre, gaining a scandalous reputation, not wholly faded. The profit of the promoter, **Edward Shepherd**, is to be conjectured in the large mansion he built for himself in Curzon St. Bought after Shepherd's death by the Marquess of Crewe, it is a superb example of a Georgian country house, with a formal garden in the midst of an urban environment. Shepherd Market now has no street stalls, but many little shops, attractive pubs and restaurants.

Buses 2, 14, 16, 19, 22, 25, 26, 30, 36, 38, 73, 74. Underground Hyde Park Corner.

Soho

2 H3

W1 The name comes from a huntsman's cry in the days when foxes thrived in the area. Now it is London's famous – sometimes infamous – cosmopolitan patch of sex shows, restaurants and continental shops. Perhaps not the place for a family outing by night, but in daytime it can be attractive. From the late 17th century onwards Soho became a refuge for French Protestants, Italians and Greeks. The individuality and zest of these people still flourish and their national character survives in the food shops, cafés and restaurants specializing in the dishes of many countries, the Chinese in **Gerrard St.** being the latest arrivals.

The web of narrow streets and still narrower alleys leads eventually to the north-east corner and **Soho Square**, a spacious area laid out in the early 17th century, now with a pleasant central garden, where Italian women and their children gather on warm summer evenings. Two churches stand in the square – one for French Protestants, the other Roman Catholic. On the corner with Greek St. is the **House of St Barnabas**, a typical Georgian mansion containing interesting relics of early Soho.

Buses 7, 8, 14, 19, 22, 25, 38, 73. Underground Oxford Circus, Piccadilly Circus or Tottenham Ct Rd.

HOLBORN, BLOOMSBURY & STRAND

These districts are the oldest outside the City of London and Westminster, a natural expansion of London as the population increased. Holborn attracted the middle classes, with modest houses, taverns and shops catering for travellers on the highways to the north and west of the country. Bloomsbury was a later development when 18th-century aristocrats bought up large tracts of land and built themselves town houses. The large squares with central gardens have largely survived. The Strand, as its name implies, ran close to the bank of the Thames, with fine houses backed by gardens gently sloping to the water.

To explore these districts it is simplest to regard the whole area as roughly a rectangle, bordered on the east by the City boundary; on the west by Charing Cross Rd and Tottenham Court Rd; on the north by Euston Rd; on the south by the Thames. Dividing the area in half horizontally is New Oxford St., which becomes High Holborn to the east.

Entering the area at St Giles Circus (the intersection of Charing Cross Rd, Tottenham Ct Rd, Oxford St., and New Oxford St.), Bloomsbury lies to the left,

Soho food store

A Strand theatre

and the British Museum and the University of London are just a few minutes' walk. Further east, past the intersection of New Oxford St., High Holborn, Kingsway and Southampton Row, Lincoln's Inn lies to the right and farther on Gray's Inn is on the left.

The Strand is best reached from Trafalgar Sq. Past Charing Cross any of the narrow roads on the left lead to Covent Garden. The end of the Strand brings one to the Savoy Chapel and Somerset House, and in the curve of Aldwych are India House and Australia House. Beyond Aldwych are the Law Courts and the 'gateway' to the City at Temple Bar.

Adelphi

WC2 Tucked away south of the Strand, this area of narrow streets was designed by the **Adam** brothers in the mid-18th century. The **Royal Society of Arts**, 8 Adam St., has a fine conference hall.
Buses 1, 6, 9, 11, 13, 15, 17. Underground Embankment or Charing Cross.

Australia House   2 K3

Aldwych WC2 The finest of the Commonwealth buildings in London, built between 1911-18. The interior is finished in woods and stone brought from Australia. There are a conference library, reading room and facilities for Australians to meet fellow countrymen.
Buses 1, 4, 6, 9, 11, 13, 15, 55, 68, 77. Underground Temple.

British Crafts Centre

42 Earlham St. WC2 Contemporary crafts for display and sale. (Buses and Underground as for Covent Garden.)

British Museum see p. 47

British Museum see p. 47

British Telecom Tower   2 H2

Maple St. W1 (Post Office Tower) Transmits TV and radio telephone signals. The Tower is 189m/620ft high. It is now closed to the public.
Buses 14, 18, 24, 27, 29, 30, 73. Underground Warren St.

Bush House

Aldwych WC2 This large office block was completed in 1931 and named after Irving T. Bush, an American businessman, to symbolize friendship between the English-speaking peoples.
(Buses and Underground as for Australia House.)

Charing Cross   6 J4

Strand WC2 In the forecourt of the station is a replica of the last of the thirteen crosses **Edward I** set up in the 13th century to mark the resting places when his Queen's body was brought from Harby, Nottinghamshire, for burial in Westminster Abbey. The original cross stood on the spot in Trafalgar Sq. now occupied by the statue of Charles I. Charing Cross is the centre of London, from which all distances in Britain are measured.

Buses 1, 3, 6, 9, 11, 12, 13, 15, 24, 29, 39, 53, 59, 77, 88. Underground Embankment or Charing Cross.

Coram's Fields   2J2

WC1 This large playground, from which adults are banned unless accompanied by children, was the site of the Foundling Hospital, built in the 18th century by Thomas Coram for the care of destitute children. **Handel** trained the children's choir and **Hogarth** used some of the children as models in his pictures. Hospital and school were moved to the countryside in 1926 and the buildings demolished. The art treasures are housed at 40 Brunswick Sq. (adjacent).

Mon.-Fri 1000–1600. Buses 17, 18, 45, 46, 68, 77. Underground Russell Sq.

Covent Garden   2J3

WC2 London's fruit and vegetable market was removed from here in 1974 to a new site at Nine Elms, Vauxhall, and all of the old warehouses and commercial premises have been demolished. It is now a thriving area of restaurants, clothing boutiques, book and music shops, craft centres, and a host of specialist traders with wares difficult or impossible to obtain elsewhere. The maze of streets, many free from traffic, offers interest no matter what one's tastes. The accent is on modest prices. Here you can buy oriental foods, eat an American meal to the accompaniment of rock music, buy a harp or a second-hand guitar, have jewellery designed to order or learn how to dance. The 'Garden' also includes the **London Transport Museum** (p. 52) and the **Theatre Museum** (p. 25).

Buses 1, 6, 9, 11, 13, 15, 24, 29, 77. Underground Covent Garden.

Ely Place

EC1 To the north of Holborn Circus, this quiet little cul-de-sac is unique in that legally it is not part of any London district and the police have no powers to enter it without permission from the beadle at the gate. It was the property of the Bishops of Ely, in whose palace **John of Gaunt** died in 1399. The only remaining ancient building is **St Etheldreda's church**, a beautiful example of 14th-century architecture lovingly restored in recent years. It is Catholic, and the first pre-Reformation church to be restored to the authority of Rome.

Buses 8, 17, 18, 22, 25, 45, 46, 63. Underground Farringdon.

Freemasons' Hall   2K3

Great Queen St. WC2 An impressive

Law Courts

Lincoln's Inn

building, dominated by a 61-m/200-ft tower, it is the HQ of the United Grand Lodge of England and serves as a war memorial to Freemasons who died in World War I.

Buses 7, 8, 19, 22, 25, 38, 55, 68, 77. Underground Holborn.

Gray's Inn 2K2

WC1 One of the four Inns of Court in London, this has been the home and workplace of lawyers since the 14th century. Severely damaged by bombing, most of the buildings have been restored, using all of the surviving original material. The large oriel window of the Hall was the gift of the American Bar Association in 1951. The gardens are beautiful and must still be much as they were when Samuel Pepys and Charles Lamb loved to walk in them. The ornamental catalpa trees are said to have been grown from cuttings brought from America by **Sir Walter Raleigh** and planted by **Francis Bacon**, Elizabethan statesman and philosopher.

Buses 8, 17, 18, 19, 22, 25, 38, 45, 46, 55. Underground Chancery Lane.

India House 2K3

Aldwych WC2 The office for the High Commissioner of the Republic of India has an interior decorated in Indian style. There are reference rooms, library, cinema and displays of Indian crafts and art.

(Buses and Underground as for Australia House)

Law Courts 2K3

Strand WC2 Officially known as the **Royal Courts of Justice**, this conglomerate of buildings, erected in 1874–82 and extended in 1968, is notable for its fine central hall. During the law terms when the courts are sitting, the public is admitted Mon.-Fri. 1000–1300 and 1400–1600 to the various courts.

Buses 1, 4, 6, 9, 11, 13, 15, 55, 68, 77. Underground Temple.

Lincoln's Inn 2K3

WC2 Another of London's Inns for the legal profession, Lincoln's Inn has been in existence since the 14th century. The Old Hall was built in 1491 and has been carefully restored. **Dickens** knew it well; he was a junior clerk in a solicitor's office here for a short time in 1827 and described the Hall in *Bleak House*. The chapel, whose foundation stone was laid by the poet **John Donne**, in 1620, has a fine interior, with a 17th-century glass window, restored after bomb damage from a Zeppelin raid in 1915. Splintered stonework on the exterior marks this early example of modern warfare. Near the west entrance to the Inn is the New Hall, built in 1843. The adjacent library contains

more than 80,000 books on the law.

Beyond the Inn is **Lincoln's Inn Fields**, largest of London's garden squares. Several museums are in the fine buildings surrounding the square, notably **Sir John Soane's Museum** (see p. 55) and that of the **Royal College of Surgeons** (see p. 55). The north side of the Fields is dedicated to the **Royal Canadian Air Force**, which had its HQ in the square during World War II. The flourishing maple tree was the gift of the City of Ottawa in 1945.

Buses 8, 22, 25, 55, 68, 77. Underground Holborn.

Old Curiosity Shop 2K3

Portsmouth Street WC2 Just beyond the south-west corner of Lincoln's Inn Fields, this much photographed 16th-century antique and souvenir shop was actually a dairy when cows grazed in the Fields. The original, described by Dickens, is believed to have stood behind the National Portrait Gallery.

(Transport as for Lincoln's Inn)

Post Office Tower see p. 97
Roman Bath

Strand Lane WC2 In a narrow street south of Aldwych is a bath fed by a natural spring. If it *was* ever used by the Romans, the existing construction is no older than the 15th century, but the lead pipes chan-

nelling the water are considerably older. (Transport as for Australia House)

Royal Opera House 2J3

Covent Garden WC2 The home of opera and ballet has seats for 2000, and is more than a century old. Three earlier theatres stood on the site, the first, opened in 1732, was taken over by Handel for his operas. Later, David Garrick was among the actors who appeared on its stage. Destroyed by fire in 1808, it was replaced by a larger building and named the Royal Italian Opera House. Again fire broke out, and the theatre was rebuilt, much as it stands today, in 1858. The portico and some sculptured panels are relics of the second (1809) building.

Buses 1, 6, 9, 11, 13, 15, 24, 29, 77. Underground Covent garden.

St Clement Danes 2K3

Strand WC2 This church was built by **Wren** in 1681, with a steeple added in 1719 to house the bells pealing out 'oranges and lemons', the nursery rhyme tune. The church was virtually destroyed by air raids, but carefully restored in 1958 to serve as the central church of the **Royal Air Force**. The metal of the original bells was re-cast in 1958 by the same founders who had made the first bells nearly four centuries earlier. On the floor are the crests of many squadrons of the RAF and

British Telecom Tower (Post Office Tower)

St Pancras Station

allied Air Forces. There is also a roll of honour of the 125,000 airmen and women who died in two world wars. An organ is the contribution of the US Air Forces, a font from the Royal Norwegian Air Force, and, in the crypt, an altar from the Royal Netherlands Air Force. Under one gallery is the US Air Force shrine, with floor carvings commemorating the Commonwealth Air Forces.

Buses 1, 4, 6, 9, 11, 13, 15, 68, 77. Underground Temple.

St Pancras Station 2J1

Euston Road NW1 This rail terminus deserves mention as an example of the extravagant ideas in the heyday of steam transportation. Built just over a century ago, the enormous building is a mixture of Italian and French Gothic styles, with an intended touch of Scottish castle (to advertise the train service to Scotland). The freight and warehouse section to the west is the site of the new **British Library** which will house most of the books used by students and researchers at the British Museum. Books will be despatched to the museum via a ½-mile tunnel.

Buses 14, 17, 18, 30, 45, 63, 73, 77. Underground King's Cross.

St Paul's

Covent Garden WC2 The church 'with the front at the back', as it is popularly known, was built by **Inigo Jones** in 1633 and described by him as 'the handsomest barn in England'. It is known as the **actors' church**, and Bernard Shaw set his first scene in *Pygmalion* (filmed as *My Fair Lady*) on the steps of the church, then a popular spot for flower sellers. (Buses and Underground as for Covent Garden)

Savoy Chapel

Savoy Hill WC2 Down a steep lane from the Strand, near Waterloo Bridge, this chapel was built in 1505 and rebuilt after a fire in 1864. It was originally the private chapel of the sovereign under his or her title of Duke of Lancaster (never Duchess), and is now the chapel of the **Royal Victorian Order**. Memorials include those to Queen Mary (consort of George V), George VI and the Duke of Kent (died 1942).

Buses 1, 4, 6, 9, 11, 13, 15, 68, 77. Underground Charing Cross.

Somerset House see p. 56

Somerset House see p. 56

Staple Inn 2K3

Holborn WC1 The gabled and timber-framed houses, built in 1586, are the last surviving examples of domestic Tudor buildings in London. They screen a court yard, originally the site of a hostel and market place for merchants of the staple (traders in wool) in the 14th century. The

area became an **Inn of Chancery** a century later and remained so until the Victorian era. Almost totally destroyed by a bomb, it has been carefully restored as an oasis of quiet charm. The Inn now houses the Institute of Actuaries.
Buses 8, 17, 18, 22, 25, 45, 46. Underground Chancery Lane.

Temple Bar

Strand WC2 This marks the boundary between Westminster and the City. The present statuary of Queen Victoria and the Prince of Wales (later Edward VII), with the City's heraldic dragon on the top, was erected in 1880 after the old gateway was removed and re-erected in Theobalds Park, Hertfordshire (near Waltham Cross). A gateway stood here at least as early as the 12th century, with spikes on which the heads of traitors and criminals were impaled after execution. When the sovereign visits the City he or she always stops at Temple Bar for ritual permission to enter from the Lord Mayor.
(Buses and Underground as for Law Courts)

University of London   2J2

Malet Street WC1 Opened in 1836 as an examining body, it became a teaching university in 1900. The main building, the Senate House, dominated by a massive tower, includes a large library especially rich in Elizabethan works.
Buses 14, 24, 29, 73, 77. Underground Russell Sq.

KENSINGTON & CHELSEA

The major attraction in Kensington is the group of museums in Exhibition Rd, which runs north to south between Kensington Rd and Cromwell Rd, giving access to the Science, Geological, Natural History, and Victoria and Albert Museums. They can also be reached from Brompton Rd. North of Exhibition Rd, beside Kensington Gardens, are the Albert Hall and Albert Memorial. A short distance west, past Queen's Gate, is Kensington High St., a busy area of large department stores, boutiques and antique shops. Beyond the shopping area the Commonwealth Institute in Holland Park lies on the right, and further on there is Olympia.

Chelsea, in the 18th century a modish residential area, subsequently favoured by writers and artists, extends south to the banks of the Thames. A good starting place is Sloane Sq. West from there the King's Rd, with the most modern fashion and novelty shops in London, is a long thoroughfare, appropriately terminating in World's End. Halfway along, roads on the left lead to Cheyne Walk, with Chelsea Old Church overlooking the Thames.

Royal Albert Hall and base of Albert Memorial

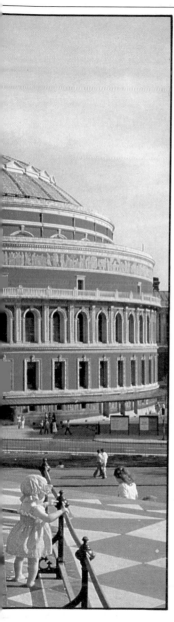

Returning east, where the road curves away from the river, are the spacious grounds of Chelsea Royal Hospital. From there one can return to Sloane Sq. or continue north east to Victoria.

Albert Hall   4D4

Kensington Gore SW7 Officially known as the Royal Albert Hall, this oval amphitheatre was completed in 1871. It can seat up to 8500 people, and the floor area can be adapted for boxing matches, conferences, displays, and dancing in addition to its normal use as a concert hall. Musical programmes are presented throughout the year. The most famous are the **Promenade Concerts** held every week night in late summer and autumn to popularize the best orchestral music, classical and modern. The 'promenaders' pay very low prices to stand and walk close to the orchestra and are mostly young enthusiasts.

Buses 9, 52, 73. Underground South Kensington.

Albert Memorial   4D4

Kensington Gore SW7 The memorial was completed shortly after the Albert Hall, at the express wish of **Queen Victoria** as a national monument to her consort, and its ornate Gothic style is characteristically Victorian. There are 178 reliefs of writers and artists around the pedestal, and at the corners figures symbolizing Industry, Engineering, Commerce and Agriculture, with other figures representing the world's continents. The bronze figure of Prince Albert shows him holding the catalogue of the Great Exhibition he inspired and supervised in neighbouring Hyde Park.

(Buses and Underground as for Albert Hall)

Brompton Oratory   4E5

Brompton Rd SW7 The building, reminiscent of Italian churches, was completed in 1884 as a tribute to **Cardinal Newman**, whose statue stands in the courtyard. The dome, 61m/200ft high, was added in 1896. In the interior are statues of the Apostles brought from Siena cathedral, and in the Lady Chapel the altarpiece came from Brescia. A relic of St Philip – the church's actual name is the London Oratory of St Philip Neri – is preserved beneath the altar in the saint's chapel.

Buses 14, 30, 74. Underground Knightsbridge or South Kensington.

Chelsea Old Church

Cheyne Walk SW3 A 12th-century church almost completely destroyed in 1941, but the south chapel, built by **Sir Thomas More**, survived. Among the memorial tablets is one to the American

author **Henry James**, who died in nearby Cheyne Row in 1916. The main part of the church was completely restored by 1958. According to legend, **Henry VIII** secretly married Jane Seymour in the church, ahead of his official formal wedding – and within 24 hours of his previous wife Anne Boleyn being beheaded.
Buses 19, 39. Underground Sloane Sq.

Chelsea Physic Garden
Royal Hospital Rd SW3 This herbal garden has probably existed since the 16th century, and was taken over by the **Society of Apothecaries** in 1673. Here were grown the cotton plants to produce seed sent to America in 1732 – the origin of the cotton-growing industry of the Southern States. It is now a centre of plant research. Open to visitors mid-Apr.–mid.-Oct. 1400–1700.
Bus 39. Underground Sloane Sq.

Commonwealth Institute
see p. 49

Crosby Hall
Cheyne Walk SW3 Now a residential hall of the **Federation of University Women**, once part of the 15th-century mansion of Sir John Crosby, a wool merchant. It was removed to its present site in 1910 to save it from demolition. Among the many treasures is one of the three copies **Holbein** made of his masterpiece *Sir Thomas More and his Family*. Open weekdays 1000–1200, 1415–1700.
Buses 19, 39. Underground Sloane Sq.

Earl's Court   4C6
Warwick Rd SW5 One of the largest reinforced concrete buildings in the world when it was opened in 1937, this hall is used for exhibitions. It can be quickly converted into a huge swimming pool.
Buses 31, 74. Underground Earl's Court.

Fulham Palace
SW6 The official residence of the **Bishop of London** until 1973. Only the courtyard is old – 16th century. The moat which used to surround the palace is now a garden.
Buses 14, 30, 39. Underground Putney Bridge.

Geological Museum see p. 50
Hyde Park Gate   4D4
SW7 This wide road of fine residential houses is famous for No. 28, the London home of **Sir Winston Churchill** and where he died in 1965.
Buses 9, 52, 73. Underground Knightsbridge.

Natural History Museum
see p. 54

Olympia   4A5
Hammersmith Rd W14 Exhibition build-

1909 Rolls-Royce in the Science Museum

George Inn on the south bank of the river

ing used mostly for commercial shows. Buses 9, 27, 28, 33, 49, 73. Underground Kensington (Olympia) during shows.

Royal Hospital Museum
see p. 55

Science Museum see p. 55

Victoria and Albert Museum
see p. 56

SOUTH OF THE THAMES

Places of interest in Central London south of the Thames are for the most part close to the river and easily reached by crossing the nearest bridge.

Bankside 3M4

SE1 The stretch of river between Blackfriars and Southwark Bridges, now dominated by a modern power station and warehouses, was an area of theatres, pleasure gardens, bear pits and brothels until the 17th century. Close to the south side of Southwark Bridge a wall tablet marks the site of the **Globe Theatre**, where many of **Shakespeare's** plays were presented, with the author among the actors. A short stroll to the river's edge provides a fine view of St Paul's and the church steeples among the new office blocks of the City.
Buses 17, 18, 76, 95, 109, 141, 149, 176. Underground Blackfriars or Mansion House.

County Hall 6K4

SE1 At the south end of Westminster Bridge was the HQ of the **Greater London Council**, built between 1912 and 1974. The library contains 95,000 books on the history of London and local government. Prints of London scenes and maps are on sale to visitors. Admission by appointment only (apply to the Librarian). Buses 12, 53, 59, 76, 109, 149, 155, 170. Underground Waterloo or Westminster.

George Inn 3M4

Borough High St. SE1 The only tavern with a **gallery** to survive in London. The original inn, patronized by pilgrims on the way to Canterbury, was burned down in 1676, after which the present building was erected. Its heyday came with the development of stage coach routes. **Dickens** mentions the tavern in *Little Dorritt*. Buses 10, 21, 40, 95. Underground London Bridge.

Lambeth Palace 6K5

Lambeth Rd SE1 Just south of Lambeth Bridge, the London residence of the **Archbishops of Canterbury** for seven centuries stands on the site of a Saxon manor house which became a Benedictine monastery after the Norman Conquest. Extensively altered and extended over the years, the palace suffered considerable

damage in World War II. Prior permission from the Chaplain is normally required to visit the nonresidential part.
Buses 10, 44, 149. Underground Westminster (near).

National Film Theatre   6K4
South Bank SE1 There are two cinemas in this building, showing films of artistic merit, and a bookstall with magazines and books on film production. Although it is a cinema club, a visitor's membership for one week or one month is available. The London Film Festival is held here Nov.-Dec.
Buses 1, 4, 68, 70, 76, 149, 171, 176, 188. Underground Waterloo.

National Theatre   6K4
South Bank SE1 This complex has three theatres – the **Olivier** with an open stage projecting into the auditorium; the **Lyttelton** with a conventional stage; and the **Cottesloe**, mainly used for experimental productions. There are buffets, bars and a restaurant within the extremely modernistic building completed in 1976.
(Buses and Underground as for National Film Theatre)

Old Vic   6L4
Waterloo Rd SE1 Victorian theatre famous this century for music, opera and drama, especially Shakespeare. Closed 1982, restored by Canadian businessman, Ed Mirvish, and reopened 1983. Policy is to present high quality musicals and drama. Subscription scheme offers discount on normal ticket prices. Opposite, in The Cut, the **Young Vic** performs plays of particular appeal to younger audiences.
Buses 1, 4, 68, 70, 76, 188. Underground Waterloo.

Oval, The
Kennington SE11 The famous ground of the **Surrey Cricket Club**, and the venue for the final Test Match between England and Commonwealth countries.
Buses 3, 36, 59, 95, 109, 133. Underground Oval.

Queen Elizabeth Hall   6K4
South Bank SE1 This hall seats 1100 for concerts by international artists. Adjacent is the **Purcell Room** for recitals.
(Transport as for National Film Theatre)

Royal Festival Hall   6K4
South Bank SE1 Often regarded as the finest example of postwar architecture in London, this hall, built in 1951, holds an audience of 3400. The stage can accommodate the largest orchestras, a choir of up to 250, or large ballet companies. The restaurant and entrance halls give splendid views across the river.
(Buses and Underground as for National Film Theatre)

Lambeth Palace

Scene from The Merry Wives of Windsor

Shell Centre
York Road SE1 One of the largest office buildings in Europe, the Centre includes a 26-floor tower, 107m/351ft high.
(Buses and Underground as for National Film Theatre)

Southwark Cathedral 3N4
London Bridge SE1 The finest Gothic building in London with the exception of Westminster Abbey, the cathedral stands on the site of a 7th-century nunnery. The interior is impressive and beautiful. Of special interest to American visitors is the **Harvard Chapel**, dedicated in 1907 to the memory of John Harvard, founder of the university, who was baptized in the church in 1607. The east window was painted by John la Farge, the American artist. Many allusions to Shakespeare, whose theatre stood close by, include a reclining figure of the dramatist below a stained glass window portraying figures from his plays.
Buses 10, 18, 21, 35, 40, 43, 44, 47, 48, 70, 95. Underground London Bridge.

LONDON'S RIVER
Until the 19th century the Thames was the most important route for passengers and freight between Westminster, the City and the royal palace at Greenwich. Today there is no better way to get the 'feel' of both historic and modern London than to take a trip on the river launches which ply from Westminster and Charing Cross Piers, downstream to the Tower and Greenwich, upstream to Richmond and Hampton Court. A slower but equally rewarding tour is to stroll along the Victoria Embankment, South Bank, Bankside or Chelsea Embankment, each of which offers about half an hour of easy exercise and sights of interest wherever you look. For the really energetic the towpath offers a 26km/16mi walk from Putney to Hampton Court (the path changes sides at Kingston).

Albert Bridge
Linking Chelsea and Battersea, this is of interest to engineers as a Victorian idea for combining suspension and cantilever bridges in one construction. Its attractive appearance, however, does not compensate for its unsuitability for today's heavy traffic, and use by vehicles is restricted.
Bus 39. Underground Sloane Sq.

Battersea Bridge
A strictly utilitarian bridge coping with the traffic which would otherwise use the Albert Bridge. It replaced a far more picturesque – but unfortunately insecure – wooden bridge which appears in paintings by **Turner** and **Whistler**.
Buses 19, 39, 45, 49. Underground Fulham Broadway.

Blackfriars Bridge   3L3

Connecting the City with Southwark, this bridge was built more than a century ago and widened in 1908. It is probably on the site of a ferry in use in Roman times as, close to the north end, part of a Roman vessel, berthed at the bank, was excavated. Buses 17, 45, 63, 76. Underground Blackfriars.

Chelsea Bridge

One of the most attractive of London's bridges, this is a suspension bridge with a 213-m/700-ft span. On the north side is an embankment walk which extends for 1.6km/1mi as far as Battersea Bridge. Bus 137. Underground Sloane Sq.

Docklands   3O4

London's new business, residential and cultural centre in process of completion downstream from Tower Bridge in the area which was once Europe's largest port and shipbuilding centre. It includes the World Trade Centre, conference halls, a marina with historic ship collection, luxury apartments and groups of more modest dwellings, a 4-star hotel on the waterfront, and a shopping piazza. Driverless computer-controlled trains afford a spectacular view of Docklands on a route from Tower Hill to the Isle of Dogs, with an extension to the London City airport (air traffic restricted to business and special flights). The museum in Docklands is scheduled to open in late 1988 to record the history of the area. Notable old warehouses and taverns have been preserved; among the latter is the Dickens Inn. Buses 22A, 56. Underground Tower Hill, light railway from Tower Hill (the Minories) to Island Gardens.

Hungerford Bridge

Now only a footway running alongside Charing Cross Rail Bridge — built to bring rail travel from the south into the heart of London — Hungerford Bridge is a quick and easy way to reach Waterloo station and the South Bank complex of theatres and concert halls. The original was a suspension bridge, and some of the sections were used to build the Clifton Suspension Bridge near Bristol. Hungerford is derived from 'Ingleford' (the ford of the Angles), indicating that there may have been a ford across the river at this point in pre-Norman times. Buses 109, 155, 171. Underground Embankment or Waterloo.

Lambeth Bridge   6J5

Linking south Westminster with south London, Lambeth Bridge stands at the spot where for many years there was a ferry operated by horses – hence Horseferry Rd on the Westminster side. The

Lambeth Bridge

Lightship in St Katharine's Dock

present bridge was largely rebuilt in 1932. Buses 3, 10, 77. Underground Westminster or Lambeth North.

London Bridge 3N4

A modern bridge which was completed in 1972. Its predecessor was demolished and re-erected as a tourist attraction at Lake Havasu City, Arizona. Until 1749 there was no other bridge linking the City with the south side of the river. The Romans had what was probably a pontoon bridge on the site, and traces of a landing stage were found in 1982. A wooden bridge was erected in the 10th century and replaced by a stone bridge in 1209. It was a spectacular achievement for the time, and there were shops on either side of the narrow roadway, a chapel in the middle, and gates at either end to guard the City from attack. The spikes on the gates were used to display the heads of executed traitors. The 19 piers of the bridge interrupted the flow of the river, causing the water to spread far wider than it now does, as far as Chelsea. A new bridge was erected in 1832, and this was the one bought for the USA. The present bridge is of pre-stressed concrete. On the City side is a short flight of steps ending in the water. These are Nancy's Steps, in Dickens' *Oliver Twist*.

Buses 10, 21, 35, 40, 43, 44, 47, 48. Underground London Bridge or Monument.

Pool of London 3N4

This is the stretch of water between London Bridge and Tower Bridge where for centuries trading vessels loaded and unloaded their merchandise at wharves in use since Saxon times. The riverside was the site of the Billingsgate fish market established in 1699 (closed in 1982). It is now being developed to provide offices, shops, and a restaurant, with a riverbus landing stage. Completion is due in 1985. The adjacent **Custom House** is early 19th century. The first customs office on this site originated in the 14th century. (Buses and Underground as for London Bridge)

Ships

HMS Belfast, moored on the south side in the Pool of London, is a Royal Navy cruiser which escorted the World War II Arctic convoys to Russia and started the bombardment of enemy coast on D-Day. It is open to the public 3N4 (Buses and Underground as for Tower Bridge)

HMS Chrysanthemum, moored on the north bank opposite the Temple, was a sloop in World War I and is now a training ship of the Royal Naval Volunteer Reserve. 3K3

MS Wellington

HMS President, next to *Chrysanthemum*, is an RN Reserve training ship.   **3L3**

Kathleen and May schooner, an 85-year-old wooden 3-masted topsail schooner, the last survivor of its type. Exhibition on board. Enclosed dock at end of Cathedral St. SE1.
Buses as for London Bridge. Underground London Bridge.

HMS Wellington is the livery hall of the Honourable Company of Master Mariners.
Buses 108, 155, 168, 184.

South Bank   6K4
London's spacious riverside promenade, stretching between Westminster Bridge and Waterloo Bridge. Despite rather austere design this is a restful area with plenty of seats and it offers the opportunity to take in the panorama of London.
Buses 1, 4, 5, 12, 53, 76, 149, 168, 171.

Waterloo Bridge

Southwark Bridge   3M3
A strictly utilitarian bridge rebuilt in 1914–21. It is the most convenient way to reach Bankside from the City.
Buses 18, 95, 149. Underground Mansion House.

Thames Barrier
The world's largest moveable flood barrier opened in 1984 downstream from Woolwich. Exhibition centre and boat trips round the barrier. Daily 1030–1700. Boats from Westminster Pier and Greenwich Pier.

Tower Bridge   3O4
One of London's most popular tourist attractions, the most spectacular of the river's bridges was opened for traffic in 1894. The ornate Gothic-style towers conceal a steel structure. Each of the **drawbridges** weighs 1000 tons and can be raised or lowered in 90 seconds — these days by electric motors but the old hydraulic engines are kept as a standby. The walkways have been renovated and are open to the public, affording fine views of the river and City. There is a small museum at the approach to the bridge, and adjacent on the north side a group of historic ships in St. Katherine's Dock.
Buses 42, 78. Underground Tower Hill.

Tower Bridge

Vauxhall Bridge   6J6
Erected in 1806, a bridge of little note beyond its sculptures representing the Arts and Sciences.
Buses 2, 36, 77, 78.

Victoria Embankment   3K3
A pleasant walk for a little over 1.6km / 1mi by day or after twilight is the stretch between Westminster Bridge and Blackfriars Bridge. On the far side of the road it is possible to walk most of the way through public gardens. To the west of

Victoria Embankment

Westminster Bridge the ornate red-brick building, Norman Shaw House, was New Scotland Yard until the Metropolitan Police HQ moved to Victoria, in 1967. North east is **Cleopatra's Needle**, inaccurately named, as it stood at Heliopolis 3500 years before the Queen of Egypt lived. (Its twin stands in Central Park, New York.) Near the end of the Embankment the entrance to the City is marked by two heraldic animals, usually described as griffins, but actually portraying dragons. (Buses and Underground as for Waterloo and Westminster Bridges)

Waterloo Bridge 6K4

Regarded as the most beautiful of London's bridges, it was completed in 1945, a minor triumph of construction while London was suffering from years of air raids. On the north side is the front and terrace of Somerset House (p. 56) seen as it was intended, not from the rear on the Strand side as it usually is. From the middle of the bridge one obtains what is possibly the best view of both Westminster and the City.
Buses 1, 4, 68, 171, 176, 188. Underground Embankment, Temple or Waterloo.

Westminster Bridge 8J4

At low tide the Thames is comparatively shallow at this point and there is reason to believe that in Roman and pre-Norman times it could be forded, though the river was then far wider. It was the second bridge to be built, after London Bridge, and while standing on it one September day in 1802 **Wordsworth** was inspired to write his famous sonnet beginning 'Earth has not anything to show more fair'. The view is still memorable. The present bridge, of cast iron, was built in 1862. At the north end is a large, symbolic statue of **Boadicea** in her chariot, erected in 1902.
Buses 12, 53, 59, 76, 77, 109, 155, 170. Underground Westminster.

LONDON'S PARKS & OPEN SPACES

Few large cities are so generously endowed with open spaces – 'the city's lungs' – as London. The parks in the central area are for the most part the property of the Crown and open to everyone. Londoners make ample use of their parks which offer the visitor a chance to see the people at rest and play.

Battersea Park

SW11 Just over a century ago this was marshland. Vast quantities of soil brought from excavations at the docks below Tower Bridge transformed the area into a park bordering the river. There are facilities for sports and games, a boating lake, amusements and a children's zoo. The park also has a **heliport** for bird's-eye tours over London and for private journeys.

Buses 19, 39, 44, 170. Underground to South Kensington or Sloane Sq., then bus.

Bushy Park and Hampton Court Park

Teddington, Middlesex A road separates these two royal parks. Bushy Park was laid out in the 17th century and is famous for its avenue of chestnuts first planted by Wren. Deer graze in its grassy spaciousness. There is a boating pool for children and facilities for games. Hampton Court Park is more formal, as Cardinal Wolsey and Henry VIII intended. A golf course, model boat pond, and flower beds are among the features, and the famous **maze** is unique.

Buses 111, 131, 152, 201, 206, 211, 216. British Rail Hampton Court.

Green Park 5G4

SW1 Bordered by Piccadilly and Constitution Hill, the land for this royal park was originally bought by **Charles II** so that he could stroll freely among his subjects. It is maintained in a natural state, with grass below many varieties of trees, and is a favourite place for al fresco meals or simply to laze away a sunny afternoon.

Buses 2, 9, 14, 16, 19, 22, 25, 26, 30, 36, 38, 52, 73, 74. Underground Green Park.

Greenwich Park

SE10 The first of the royal parks to be enclosed – in 1433. It is 'the centre of the world' for it has the **Meridian Line** marking zero degrees of longitude. Formal beds of flowers contrast with woodland glens and copses. A bird sanctuary, tennis courts, a children's play area, and ornamental ponds are attractions, but perhaps the most memorable feature is the panoramic view of London from the upper slopes.

Buses 53, 54, 75, 177. British Rail Maze Hill.

Hampstead Heath

NW3 The steep escarpment north of Central London rises to 122m/400ft through trees and little glens, with wild flowers, nesting birds, and great expanses of grass, to the ancient **Spaniards Road** on the crest, from which all London and the Surrey hills far beyond can be seen. This is the Londoner's favourite place for a day out of doors within easy travelling distance. Swimming in natural pools or a well-equipped **Lido**, horse riding, jogging along winding paths or serious running on cinder tracks, kite flying, fishing, and sailing model boats are some of the popular recreations.

Buses 24, 46. Underground Hampstead.

Speakers' Corner, Hyde Park

Regent's Park

Hyde Park   4E4

W1 A dense forest and swampy marshland, the home of deer and wild boar,
made this area an almost unknown ter-
ritory to Londoners for centuries. Then
Henry VIII annexed it as Crown property
and created a hunting park. His daughter
Elizabeth I had part of it cleared for
military reviews. In the 17th century it
was opened to the public and became a
fashionable place for driving, riding and
entertainments. A stream was channelled
and dammed early in the 18th century to
form a lake, the **Serpentine**, where one
can rent sailing or rowing boats, fish, or
bathe at the Lido. **Rotten Row**, a
specially prepared horse-riding track of
sandy soil, runs round three-quarters of
the Park. To the north east is **Speakers'
Corner**, London's famous centre of free
speech, where anyone may address the
crowd on any subject provided it is not
treasonable, obscene, and does not include demands for money. Best times to
visit the Corner are Saturday evening and
all day Sunday.
Buses 2, 6, 7, 8, 9, 12, 14, 15, 16, 19, 22, 25,
26, 30, 36, 38, 52, 73, 74, 88. Underground Hyde Park Corner or Marble
Arch.

Kensington Gardens   4D4

W8 Adjacent to Hyde Park, this royal
park was developed by William III and
then by Queen Caroline, consort of
George II, in the early years of the 18th
century. The Flower Walk, Broad Walk,
Sunken Gardens, and the Round Pond are
attractions. In the **Children's Garden** is
a stunted oak carved with elves and fairies,
and beside the lake a statue of Peter Pan.
West of the road dividing Hyde Park from
Kensington Gardens is the Serpentine
Gallery, used by the Arts Council for
periodic exhibitions of contemporary art.
Buses 9, 12, 27, 28, 33, 49, 52, 73, 88.
Underground Kensington High St. or
Lancaster Gate.

Regent's Park   1F1

NW1 Henry VIII kept this area as one of
his many hunting parks. It was not opened
to the public until 1835 when it was
named in honour of the Prince Regent
(later George IV). **John Nash** designed
the layout and built the beautiful Regency
houses which fringe the east and south
sides. The displays of flowers are regarded
as the finest in London and the greatest
collection of roses in the country is to be
found in **Queen Mary's Gardens** at the
centre. Boats can be rented on the lake,
which has a bird sanctuary and heronry.
On the north side are flat areas for organized games. The **Open Air Theatre**
presents plays – usually Shakespeare's –

during the summer, and band concerts are held in the afternoon and evening. The US Ambassador's magnificent private residence, **Winfield House**, presented to the USA in 1946, is within the park's boundary.

The north-east corner is occupied by the **Zoo**, with an unexcelled collection of more than 6000 creatures, many not to be seen in any other zoo. On the Mappin terraces bears, monkeys and other animals live without bars in comparative freedom. Three of the most popular attractions are the penguin and sea-lion pools, and the lion terrace. The huge aquarium, the insect and reptile houses, the giant panda enclosure, the children's zoo with many tame animals roaming among the young visitors, and the walk-through aviary designed by Lord Snowdon are other notable features.

Buses 2, 3, 13, 26, 74. Underground Regent's Park, Camden Town or Baker St.

Richmond Park

Surrey The largest of all the royal parks was originally a hunting park for Charles I and Charles II. Several hundred red and fallow deer, the property of the Queen, still roam free among the clumps of trees, heather and bracken. Gardens and plantations are dotted here and there to blend with the natural scenery. There are two public golf courses, lakes for fishing (permit required), pitches for football, cricket and polo, and riding paths for horses. There are also a few houses in the park. **White Lodge**, George II's hunting box, was the birthplace of Edward VIII (Duke of Windsor) and is now a base for the Royal Ballet school.

Underground or British Rail, Richmond.

Richmond Park

St James's Park   5H4

SW1 The prettiest of the central royal parks includes the ancient (and still official) palace of the kings and queens of England. The fields and woodland beyond the palace were cleared, and the area walled in by Henry VIII. Elizabeth I opened up more grounds for fetes, tournaments and pageants. But it was **Charles II** who was responsible for much of its present appearance, copying parks he had seen while in exile in France. He had the lake excavated, planted exotic trees, created wide expanses of lawns, and built the wide thoroughfare, the Mall, on one side. His formal designs were partially changed by **John Nash** to give a more typically English appearance. The flower beds are the pride of the royal parks' gardeners, and the islands in the lake provide sanctuary for a wide variety of waterfowl. The park is a favourite place

Queen Elizabeth I's Hunting Lodge, Epping Fore

for Government Ministers and officials to enjoy some fresh air away from their Whitehall offices nearby, and Londoners take little notice when seeing, among the many people feeding the birds from the lake bridge, the familiar faces of a statesman or two.

Buses 3, 11, 12, 24, 29, 53, 77. Underground St James's, Charing Cross or Victoria.

IN GREATER LONDON & SUBURBS

Places of varied interest abound in the London conurbation and suburbs, and none of them more than 30 minutes by bus, train or coach from the centre. They offer a half-day outing, often in surprisingly rural surroundings.

Alexandra Park

Wood Green N22 The building on the crown of the hill was intended to be a second Crystal Palace. It was from here that the world's first regular TV programmes were transmitted, in 1936. It has been partly destroyed by fire, but the extensive grounds include children's play area, boating lakes and a ski centre (open Oct.-April).

Underground Wood Green, then bus 103.

Epping Forest

Chingford, Essex Strangely, this is legally part of the **City of London**, bought for the public benefit by the Corporation in 1878. It extends for 16km/10mi and is the remains of a huge forest kept as a royal hunting area. **Elizabeth I's Hunting Lodge** includes a small museum telling the history of the forest. Its primitive and wild beauty has attracted many writers and artists, including Tennyson and Jacob Epstein, the sculptor.

Buses 10, 20, 69, 102, 121, 145, 167, 179, 191. Underground Epping.

Epsom

Surrey Still pleasantly rural, the town was originally a spa and a favourite resort of Charles II. But since 1780 it has been famous as the site of the **Derby Stakes**, run on the racecourse on the Downs during the summer meeting at the end of May or beginning of June. Attracting tens of thousands on race days, the rolling expanse of countryside is at other times largely deserted except for ramblers and nature lovers.

British Rail Epsom or Epsom Downs.

Greenwich

SE10 The Tudor monarchs, devoted to turning England into a maritime power, made this area a royal town. Henry VIII was born here, as were his daughters Mary and Elizabeth. The old palace was rebuilt during the reigns of Charles II and William III, but was then taken over as a hospital for disabled and aged naval pensioners. In 1873 it became the **Royal Naval College** which contains the magnificent Painted Hall. Beyond the wrought iron ornamental gates linking the two parts of the college, a formal walk leads to the **Queen's House**, a miniature palace completed in time for Henrietta Maria, bride of Charles I. This is Inigo Jones's masterpiece, and it became the model for many of the much larger stately homes of England built in the 17th and 18th centuries. The palace is linked by a colonnade to the **National Maritime Museum** (p. 53).

Buses 53, 54, 75, 177, 180, 185. British Rail Maze Hill. River launches from Charing Cross or Westminster Piers.

Hampton Court

Teddington, Middlesex Without doubt the most impressive and beautiful of all the royal palaces, though no sovereign has resided there since the time of George II (1683–1760). It was built by **Cardinal Wolsey**, and had 280 rooms always prepared for guests. The palace's luxury and ostentation aroused the envy of **Henry VIII**, and tradition has it that Wolsey offered the entire place along with 400 servants to evade arrest for treason. While Henry accepted the palace, Wolsey had to accept dismissal and arrest. The king enlarged his new acquisition, and five of his wives lived in it. **Charles II** was largely responsible for laying out the extensive gardens, and soon afterwards **Wren** began rebuilding it, the result a blend of Tudor and Wren's grandiose style.

The Pond Garden, Hampton Court Palace

Passing through Wolsey's magnificent gatehouse, one comes to the largest of the three main courts round which the palace is built; this area is almost entirely early 16th century. On the east side Anne Boleyn's Gateway leads to **Clock Court**, with the astronomical clock made in 1540 and still working. On the north side is Henry VIII's **Great Hall** with a superb hammerbeam roof and, at the sides, the Tudor kitchens, wine cellars and other domestic rooms. The **State Rooms**, on the upper floor, have priceless paintings by Lely, Mantegna and Kneller.

Buses 111, 131, 152, 201, 206, 211, 216, 264, 267. British Rail Hampton Court.

Kew

Surrey For more than 200 years the **Royal Botanical Gardens** have contained the finest collection of plants in Europe. Within the grounds there are more than 45,000 different trees, shrubs and plants; the Herbarium preserves some seven million specimens, and the library has 50,000 volumes on everything that

Pagoda, Kew Gardens

grows. Although Kew's real purpose is scientific, it is a fascinating place for the visitor who can stroll among masses of flowers and rest by the river or lake. In the laboratories and glasshouses Marquis wheat was bred, which transformed Canada into a great grain-growing country; rubber trees, the source of prosperity in Malaysia, were grown from seeds rushed from the forests of Brazil; cinchona trees were grown and sent to India for the production of quinine. The huge temperate house, the hot houses and the cacti house reproduce the conditions of any desired climate. Dominating the gardens is a flagpole, 68m/225ft high a Douglas fir from British Columbia.
Buses 15, 27, 65. Underground Kew Gardens.

Wembley
Middlesex The **Stadium**, built in 1923–4 (on the site of an area where an attempt had been made to construct a replica of the Eiffel Tower), is, of course, the arena of national and international football matches, and is also used throughout the year for a variety of important spectator sports. The **Empire Pool** is used for tennis, horse jumping and ice shows, as well as for swimming. A recent addition is a large **conference centre** serving business and industrial interests.
Buses 8, 18, 83, 92. Underground Wembley Park.

Wimbledon
SW19 The courts of the **All-England Lawn Tennis and Croquet Club** gain the attention of the whole sporting world when the championships are held at the end of June. At other times the place is attractive thanks to the large **common** with woods, small lakes and heather. The **windmill** in the centre is one of the few surviving in the Home Counties. It has a museum open Sat.-Sun. 1400–1700.
Buses 28, 72, 168. Underground Wimbledon (special bus services during tennis championships).

OUT-OF-LONDON TRIPS
British Rail either goes direct to most of the places in this section, or goes to a station from which the local bus service takes you on to your chosen destination. National Express buses also offer regular services or tours. Green Line coaches run from Victoria Coach Station and Eccleston Bridge. Days of opening vary according to season. Enquiries should be made in advance at any travel agency, or the National Tourist Information Centre, Victoria Station forecourt (tel. 730 3488).

Banbury
Oxfordshire (116km/72mi) Market town of Saxon origin. Famous for Banbury

clipper, Cutty Sark, *Greenwich*

cakes (spiced currants in pastry) and for **Banbury Cross** of nursery rhyme fame. **Sulgrave Manor**, 13km/8mi north east of the town, is an Elizabethan manor house which was the home of **George Washington's** direct ancestors. The armorial bearings on the main doorway are reputedly the origin of the **Stars and Stripes** of the US flag.
British Rail from Paddington.

Bath
Avon (170km/106mi) Founded by the Romans as a spa because of its hot mineral springs, Bath is England's most elegant city, its centre largely Georgian. It also has impressive **Roman remains** and large 16th-century **abbey**. **Claverton Manor**, 3km/2mi south east, is the first **American museum** to be established outside the USA, with rooms furnished to reproduce American domestic life from 17th to 19th centuries. Part of George Washington's garden from Mount Vernon is a special exhibit.
British Rail from Paddington.

Beaulieu
Hampshire (142km/88mi) A 16th-century mansion converted from the gatehouse of a Cistercian abbey founded in 1204. The **motor museum** has the finest collection of automobiles in the country.
British Rail from Waterloo to Brockenhurst or Southampton, then bus.

Brighton
East Sussex (85km/53mi) 'London by the Sea' is notable for the **Royal Pavilion**, built for the Prince Regent (later George IV) – the exterior in the style of an Indian palace, the interior with Chinese furnishings. **The Lanes**, carefully preserved alleys of the early 19th century, are famous for antique shops. Resort attractions include a large aquarium and a museum of dolls. At **Rottingdean**, 5km/3mi away, is the **Grange Museum** of toys from all over the world.
British Rail from Victoria.

Broadstairs
Kent (122km/76mi) Quiet vacation and yachting resort best known for its links with **Charles Dickens**, who wrote *David Copperfield* while living in his 'airy nest' overlooking the harbour. The house is now named Bleak House in token of the inspiration he obtained there for his next novel. And the town holds a Dickens **festival** every summer, usually in the last week of June.
British Rail from Charing Cross.

Bury St Edmunds
Suffolk (121km/75mi) Ancient town of Norman origin with **abbey** (ruined) built as shrine for Edmund, king of East Anglia, martyred in 870. In memory of the **US**

Roman baths at Bath

Royal Pavilion, Brighton

airmen who were stationed in the vicinity during World War II there is a memorial garden in the abbey precincts. The **Gershom-Parkington Museum** has a collection of timepieces.
British Rail from Liverpool St.

Cambridge
Cambridgeshire (87km/54mi) University town of 29 colleges, with **Peterhouse** founded in 1284. **King's College chapel** is regarded as the finest example of a building in the Perpendicular style in existence. It took from 1446 to 1531 to build. Rubens' *Adoration of the Magi* is the chapel's most treasured painting.
British Rail from Liverpool St., or Green Line 798.

Canterbury
Kent (90km/56mi) The metropolitan city of the English Church since 602, with a cathedral started five years earlier. Nothing remains of the original building; the present **cathedral** dates from 1067, with additions between 1174 and 1470. About a third of the town surrounding the cathedral was laid waste by bombs during the Second World War, with the indirect result of exposing traces of Stone Age, Roman and Saxon settlements.
British Rail from Victoria or Charing Cross.

Chichester
West Sussex (98km/61mi) The importance of this town to the Romans is seen in today's streets, which are straight and cross at right angles in traditional Roman manner. Many traces of **Roman buildings** remain. The **cathedral**, founded in the 11th century, has been largely rebuilt after disastrous fires and the collapse of the tower and spire. A charming street of 18th–19th-century houses is known as **Little London** because of the wealthy residents of the capital who came to live there in the Georgian period. The **Festival Theatre**, opened in 1962, is among the country's finest theatres, and holds a festival of drama every summer.
British Rail from Waterloo or Victoria.

Chilterns, The
Buckinghamshire (34km/21mi) Area of natural beauty with many historical associations. Near Princes Risborough is **Chequers**, rural residence of the Prime Minister and scene of many conferences with US statesmen. Nearby is **Penn**, home of the ancestors of the founder of Pennsylvania. Most famous of all **Quaker** meeting houses, at **Jordans**, has gravestones of the Penn and Pennington families. At Chalfont St Giles is the house where **Milton**, fleeing from the plague in London, completed *Paradise Lost* and began *Paradise Regained*.

British Rail from Paddington to Gerrard's Cross, then local buses.

Ely

Cambridgeshire (113km/70mi)   Standing on what was once an island in an expanse of waterlogged marshes, the town was a stronghold where the English held out against invading Normans. The **cathedral**, completed in 1083 on the site of a church in existence four centuries earlier, has an octagonal **lantern tower** regarded as the finest of medieval construction.
British Rail from Liverpool St.

Hastings

East Sussex (101km/63mi)   Coastal town where **William the Conqueror** began the Norman invasion of England in 1066. The decisive battle took place 11km/7mi inland at Senlac, then renamed **Battle**. On the spot where the English king Harold fell, William built a great abbey. Thanks largely to American generosity the **abbey** ruins and **battlefield** have been preserved for posterity.
British Rail from Charing Cross or Victoria.

Hatfield

Hertfordshire (34km/21mi)   Old coaching town on the road to Scotland, and the childhood home of **Elizabeth I**. Remains of the castle in which she lived stand in the grounds of **Hatfield House**, ancestral home of the Cecil family. The **State Rooms** contain valuable paintings and tapestries, and there are many mementos of Elizabeth I, including the famous 'rainbow' portrait by Zuccaro.
British Rail from King's Cross, or Green Line 732.

Hidcote Manor

Gloucestershire (121km/75mi)   In 1905, a US army officer, Major Lawrence Johnson, drawn to the beauty of the Cotswolds, acquired a small manor house and some neglected fields with an old cedar tree and a clump of beeches. Over a period of 40 years he turned the place into what has been praised as the most beautiful **garden** created in the 20th century. There are, in fact, more than 20 gardens, each with its own style and colouring, and each cunningly designed to delight the visitor.
No train service. Nearest, Banbury or Stratford-on-Avon from Paddington, then taxi.

Knole

Kent (42km/26mi)   One of the largest private houses in England, it was built around an existing house by the Archbishop of Canterbury in the 15th century as an episcopal palace. Henry VIII commandeered it, and it was then inherited by Elizabeth I who gave it to her

Knole House, Sevenoaks

The gardens of Luton Hoo

cousin, later the Earl of Dorset. The **Sackville** family have lived there for nearly four centuries. The poet Victoria Sackville West was born in the house, which has 365 windows, 52 staircases and 7 courtyards – hence the nickname **Calendar House**. Knole is periodically open to the public; the enormous **park** is always open.

British Rail from Charing Cross to Sevenoaks, then bus.

Longleat

Wiltshire (159km/99mi) One of the largest and most impressive mansions built during the reign of Elizabeth I, with early 19th-century additions in the Italian style by the fourth **Marquess of Bath**, whose descendants have remained in possession. Among priceless treasures of paintings, furniture and books is a first folio of Shakespeare's plays. Part of the huge park has been turned into an **animal reserve**, with lions, *etc*, ranging free.

British Rail from Paddington to Westbury, then taxi.

Luton Hoo

Bedfordshire (48km/30mi) The home of the Wernher family, it is an 18th-century mansion by **Robert Adam**, remodelled in the French style. Art collection includes pictures by Rembrandt and Titian, tapestries, antique jewellery and china, and mementos of the Russian Tsars.

British Rail from St Pancras to Luton, then bus.

Oxford

Oxfordshire (88km/55mi) Ancient town which became a university city in 1167 when **Henry II** proclaimed that he wished to ensure 'there may never be wanting a succession of persons duly qualified for the service of God in Church and State'. **Bodleian Library** has three million books. In the **Museum of the History of Science** is the world's greatest collection of astronomical, optical and mathematical instruments. The 13th–15th-century church of **St Mary the Virgin** is a brass-rubbing centre.

British Rail from Paddington, or Green Line 790.

Runnymede

Near Egham, Surrey (34km/21mi) On land beside the Thames, **Magna Carta** was signed on 15 June 1215. Actual spot is marked by a granite pillar below a star-spangled dome, gift of the American Bar Association in 1957. Two other memorials stand nearby – one to the 20,455 **airmen** of the Commonwealth killed in World War II, with no known grave; the second to **John F. Kennedy**: a block of Portland stone standing on three acres of land presented to the USA. British Rail from Waterloo or Paddington then bus, or Green Line 718.

Rye

East Sussex (103km/64mi) Once a major seaport, this town is now inland owing to the sea's receding. Picturesque cobbled streets and alleys are lined with medieval houses, notably the **Mermaid Inn**, first offering food and shelter in the 13th century. **Lamb House** was the home of Henry James, the American novelist, for the last 18 years of his life. He wrote *The Wings of a Dove*, *The Golden Bowl*, and *The Ambassadors* there.
British Rail from Charing Cross to Hastings, then bus.

St Albans

Hertfordshire (34km/21mi) Major **Roman city** established in AD 43. Many medieval buildings survive, including the **Fighting Cocks** tavern, believed to be the oldest inn in the country. The **abbey**, built around the shrine of St Alban, England's first Christian martyr, is the second largest religious building in the UK. The Roman city has been excavated, and includes a theatre with a large auditorium and colonnaded stage.
British Rail from St Pancras or Euston, or Green Line 707.

Salisbury

Wiltshire (135km/84mi) The glory of this ancient town is its 13th-century **cathedral**, with the tallest spire, 123m/404ft, in England. On Salisbury Plain, 16km/10mi north, is the greatest Bronze Age monument in Europe – **Stonehenge**, a double circle of enormous stones, erected around 1500 BC, probably used for religious purposes and astronomical calculations.
British Rail from Waterloo.

Stoke Poges

Buckinghamshire (32km/20mi) The large manor house in this quiet village has numbered among its guests Elizabeth I and, less happily, Charles I as Cromwell's prisoner. Nearby is the 14th-century church with the churchyard in which **Thomas Gray** was inspired to write his famous elegy.
British Rail from Paddington to Slough, then bus.

Stratford-upon-Avon

Warwickshire (148km/92mi) Fine Tudor and Georgian town, the most popular tourist attraction outside London. To gain an idea of Shakespeare's links, start at the information centre and museum in Henley St. Then visit the reputed birthplace nearby, Holy Trinity church where he was baptized and buried, his daughter's home, his wife Anne Hathaway's cottage at Shottery, and the

Shakespeare's birthplace, Stratford-upon-Avon

Virginia Water, Windsor Great Park

Royal **Shakespeare Theatre** on the banks of the Avon. Many places of interest not connected with Shakespeare merit a visit, including the 16th-century **Harvard House**, where John Harvard, founder of the US university, was born.
British Rail from Paddington.

Warwick
Warwickshire (148km/92mi) Dominating the town is the **castle**, built on a crag above the river Avon. It is one of the few English fortified castles of the Middle Ages inhabited until this century. Much of the interior has been rebuilt, but the 14th-century defensive walls and tower remain intact. The castle is a treasure-house of paintings and furniture, and the collection of **armour** and medieval **weapons** is unique.
British Rail from Paddington.

West Wycombe
Buckinghamshire (51km/32mi) This village of 17th- and 18th-century houses, property of the National Trust, remains unspoiled by modern development, even though the A40 runs through it. The surrounding land has been the property of the Dashwood family since the 17th century. Sir Francis Dashwood formed the **Hell Fire Club**, notorious in the 18th century for its excesses, both factual and fictional. The huge park was laid out in erotic shapes, now blurred by time. On the steep hill is the roofless mausoleum with a ball-topped tower in which the club members were supposed to dine. There are caves (open periodically to the public) beneath the hill with more links with the roistering of 18th-century roués.
British Rail from Paddington to High Wycombe then bus, or Green Line 790.

Westerham
Kent (35km/22mi) A statue on the green proclaims this village as the home for many years of **Sir Winston Churchill**. His house, **Chartwell**, 3km/2mi, is preserved with the card table set up for a game of bezique, his study as it was when he last wrote there, and the studio with some of his paintings and brushes.
British Rail from Charing Cross or Victoria to Oxted then bus, or Green Line 705 (Sun. only).

Windsor
Berkshire (37km/23mi) The town is dominated by the **castle** first built by William the Conqueror and steadily enlarged and strengthened from the 12th to 19th centuries. **State Apartments** (closed when the Queen is in residence) contain magnificent paintings and furniture. **St George's Chapel**, built in 15th century for Knights of the Garter, is resplendent with heraldic devices and sculpture. In

castle precincts the **Changing of the Guard** takes place daily at 1025. The town's **Guildhall** has dioramas of Windsor's history and royal portraits. Long Walk from the castle stretches 5km/3mi through the Great Park. Nearby is Royal Windsor **safari park**.

British Rail from Paddington or Waterloo, or Green Line 701.

Wisley

Surrey (39km/24mi) The gardens and research laboratories of the **Royal Horticultural Society** are of interest as much to those who merely enjoy a peaceful time in an area of scenic beauty as they are to the horticulturist.

British Rail from Waterloo to Esher then bus, or Green Line 740.

Woburn Abbey

Bedfordshire (69km/43mi) The huge mansion of the Dukes of Bedford includes 14 **State Rooms** crammed with priceless works of art, including paintings by Canaletto, Rembrandt, van Dyck and Gainsborough. Part of the large park is an **animal reserve** with rare and exotic creatures living in a semiwild state.

British Rail from Euston to Leighton Buzzard then bus, or Green Line 737.

Woodstock

Oxfordshire (103km/64mi) This ancient town was royal property, with a palace dating from Anglo-Saxon times, where kings and queens came for hunting, and sometimes refuge in troublous periods. The Black Prince was born here and Elizabeth I was kept prisoner here as a young girl by her sister Queen Mary. What remained of the palace was demolished when **Blenheim** was built, 1705–22. Known as the 'English Versailles', this enormous palace was presented to John Churchill, first **Duke of Marlborough**, in gratitude for his victorious war over France. The contents match the magnificence of the building itself. In contrast to the grandiose appearance of most of the interior is the small room where **Sir Winston Churchill** was born to his American mother, Jenny Jerome, on 30 November 1874. Just outside the palace park, in Bladon churchyard, is a plain slab bearing the words *Winston Leonard Spencer Churchill 1874–1965*, marking the statesman's last resting place, beside his father and mother.

British Rail from Paddington to Oxford, then bus.

Blenheim Palace, Woodstock

INDEX

All place names, buildings and monuments which have a main entry are printed in heavy type. Map references also appear in heavy type and refer to Central London Maps between pages 36–46.